THE ENIGMA OF EVIL

THE
ENIGMA
OF EVIL

ALFRED SCHÜTZE

Floris Books

Translated by Eva Lauterbach from the second edition

First published in English by Floris Books in 1978
Second printing 2012
Originally published in German under the title
Das Rätsel des Bösen by Verlag Urachhaus
Second revised edition © 1969 Verlag Urachhaus, Stuttgart

British Library CIP Data available
ISBN 978-086315-860-5
Printed in Poland

Contents

The Present Situation 9

The Growth of Evil 17

Evil—the Touchstone for Freedom 32

The Two Faces of Evil 36

The many Aspects of the Fall 55

The Fall of the Intellect 60

The Nature of Evil 74

Ahrimanic Influences and Possession 78

The Coming of Antichrist 89

The Present Situation

In past epochs, the cardinal problem with which human souls had to wrestle was the mystery of death. The ancient Egyptian culture with its rites concerning the dead and the preservation of their bodies, its gigantic mausoleums and its mythology, is an example of the mystery of death as a focus of religious consciousness, before which all other questions paled. During the Greek cultural period too, great thinkers were engaged with the question of death. 'I would rather be a serf in the house of some landless man, with little enough for himself to live on, than king of all these dead men that have done with life.'* This sentence from the Eleventh Song of Homer's *Odyssey* characterizes the feeling of scepticism and tragedy which, for the Greek, was attached to the mystery of death and overshadowed life.

To our present consciousness the mystery of death has become less important than the mystery of evil. While the first question remains as one of mankind's unsolved problems, it has lost some of its urgency in view of the increasingly threatening assault of evil. In most cases we are confronted by the mystery of death only in certain life situations, as when we have lost a person close to us, or when we ourselves hear the *memento mori*. Evil, on the other hand, threatens us almost every hour of our life with continually increasing intensity.

Before going into detail, it would seem appropriate to clarify the sense in which we shall talk about evil. Our

* Translation of E. V. Rieu. Penguin Books, 1946.

starting point is not the dogmatic view developed by Christian forms of faith which consider evil mainly as deviation from religious norms. Some of what formal Church doctrine considers sinful will seem irrelevant here while different activities and conditions, not hitherto included in the category of sin, will be considered as manifestations of evil. Thus the concept will include less on the one hand and more on the other. Much of what was moral transgression in the code of the nineteenth century is outdated in view of the present acceleration of evil. At least, many of the moral deviations of those years now seem almost harmless and one is inclined to smile at them. Totally different dimensions of evil are finding outlet today. In speaking of 'evil' today we should no longer think in terms of those old catalogues of error deriving from the waning Middle Ages and we should not carry over, with all their limitations, the narrow-minded decisions of previous judges of morality.

We cannot ignore the rising number of criminal offences especially in countries of advanced culture, or the vastly increasing number of young people and children participating in crime. But of even greater concern than the number is the kind of temptations met with today. Totally new seductions and enticements threaten the moral sphere. The very foundations of moral behaviour seem to be shaken. The organ of perception of moral quality may have become so atrophied that many are not only lacking in a right feeling for the deviousness of their deeds but even boast about them. There seems to be something like a collective susceptibility to evil, and weakness in resisting it, so that even highly esteemed individuals are suddenly gripped by it even after a long and blameless life within family and profession. Many cases come to mind of espionage and bribery which were the downfall of highly placed persons—scientists, politicians and others. There is the part played by treason, which has become world-wide. Never before could one observe as one can today that educated men from sound, harmless and seemingly stable backgrounds have become susceptible in such degree. There is more involved than just a moral breakdown, which can happen anywhere and at any time.

The terrible things which have happened during the two world wars are almost forgotten. The inhuman crimes committed in the concentration camps of Nazi Germany are in process of being pushed on one side in spite of massive documentation and still on-going trials. Also fading from awareness are atrocities committed in the Russian concentration camps, in which millions perished.

New atrocities, with evil triumphant, have resulted from the wars in Korea, Vietnam, the Near East and Africa. Since the two world wars whole populations have been deported from their homelands with brutal force, sometimes for the flimsiest of reasons. One cannot even come close to estimating how much injustice and how much human misery are connected with this.

The methods of torture in the twentieth century are a particularly appalling chapter. By no means are they only applied in poorly developed countries. On the contrary, highly civilized people have also brought them to a perfection that should make us pause to think. While during antiquity and the Middle Ages, flagellation, maiming, tying to the wheel, blinding and the 'iron maiden' were used, today's tortures have different methods: skin is torn off in strips and salt water is poured into the wounds, the victims' finger nails are pulled out or iron nails are pushed under them, electric shock is applied to highly sensitive parts of the body, whereby particularly sadistic perversions occur. Apart from the executions in the concentration camps, tortures such as these and others have been committed by members of other highly developed European nations:

11

by the French in Algiers, the Dutch in Indonesia (1945 to 1950), the Greeks, as well as the North and South Vietnamese, the Koreans, etc. And what has recently been reported about the concentration camps of the Soviet Union and the gaols of Spain and South Africa can hardly be considered more humane.

A special form of torture, perfected with scientific exactitude, has come to abhorrent perfection, namely the destruction of the individual personality. Experiences gained from Pavlov's experiments with dogs are being applied to men and women. The inner breakdown of the terrorized victim is forcibly induced through systematically prompted fear and shock, intensified bodily and emotional tortures, interrogations lasting for days, accompanied by hunger, thirst, solitary confinement and deprivation of light. Under such conditions the victim is shown the only way of escape to save his physical existence and that of his soul and spirit. It consists in accepting and practising a particular doctrine which the person, broken and destroyed to his core, is made to perceive and embrace as his salvation. Attention is diverted from the brutality of such treatment by giving it the harmless-sounding term, 'brainwashing'. In many countries, such as China, this modern form of torture has been applied systematically to indoctrinate even millions of people with dialectical materialism.

In the western world less harmful methods of 're-education' are customary. The mass media, cinema, radio, TV, newspapers and periodicals work in a simpler and more elegant manner. Manipulation and levelling of people result from such procedures in both instances. Propaganda and advertising are using half-truths, lies and subliminal suggestions to direct the masses as desired at a given time.

Not lastly, some administrative and political organizations are working to deprive man of his individuality, degrade him more and more to a number only. Certainly this is not always the intention, but it is sometimes the uncontrolled side-effect of certain procedures applied without feeling and thinking. In particular, certain party doctrines, and the chauvinists and extremists of various political persuasions, are undermining respect for the human personality, destroying the concept of man and leading to inhumanity. The 'Wall' and the border between East and West Germany which is secured by barbed wire, minefields, watch towers, and guard dogs, and similar conditions in the Near East, Asia and elsewhere, show what happens when certain ideas are implemented fanatically and without regard for humanity.

People striving for freedom, literary men, artists and scientists, who do not wish to sacrifice their individuality, are a thorn in the side of bureaucracy almost everywhere in the world. Depending on the ruling régime, they are rendered harmless by the bestowal of honours, prizes and titles, or by brutal measures and—as the persecutions in Russia, Spain, Greece and China are showing—they are being shut up in gaols and asylums.

Student revolution has added a new note to the crescendo of evil in attempting to secure by terrorism the meeting of justifiable demands, and letting itself be drawn into a brutal fury of destruction. This, especially, shows that it is not enough to be right. It should be realized altogether: one may have the best ideas and intentions—but if ideas cannot be implemented in a form befitting human conditions, they become destructive. It also matters *who* has such ideas and *how* they are bedded into the whole realm of the individual's soul and spirit. There are no such things as neutral or indifferent ideas; even if they seem morally neutral at first, they almost immediately take on moral aspects. Ideas created by reason can be powerfully misused. This becomes evident above all in the technical innovations and discoveries which have led to the perfection of those terrible

13

weapons whose employment is feared by the entire world. The unfathomable temptations and dangers which can become the agents of evil at any time need not be enumerated in detail. It is sufficient to spell out the dreadfully simple word A-B-C weapons (atomic bomb—bacterial weapons—chemical warfare) in order to realize how far evil can be brought. But a particular phenomenon of evil in our time should be specially mentioned.

Whereas only a few centuries ago evil, so-called, had to be considered pertinent to moral behaviour, more specifically to the backsliding or weakness of the individual, it also appears today in a manner detached from the individual. It shows up impersonally in arrangements and conditions of social, industrial, technical and general life which, admittedly, are created and tolerated by man. It appears anonymously as injustice or hardship in an interpersonal realm where nobody seems directly liable or responsible. For example one can be caught between the millstones of bureaucratic or police regulations and no specific person can be held responsible for the inhumanity that may be suffered. Evil makes less use now of a passionate person than of an impersonal arrangement. In the times past, evil needed people who were unstable, weak in character and of questionable ethics; in our time it has created for itself a neutral plane where it can become effective in circumstances uninfluenced by emotions. The despicable 'villain' of yesterday has largely given way to the impersonal evil which may look indifferent and harmless or may work as anonymous shadow behind the scenes. The passionate, feverish evil has been replaced by the 'cold' evil, which one can also call the institutionalized evil. It has become the grey eminence infiltrating all areas of human existence and hiding behind the 'factual' and 'objective'. Through an almost imperceptible alteration of method, it can turn the best institution into its opposite or otherwise lead it to absurdity. (For example business can become totally paralysed at the post office or customs if the officials 'work to rule'.) No directly observable injustice happens; only certain situations are made senseless through literal application of regulations or other exaggerations, or they are used to turn the humane into the inhumane. In many cases it is the very harmlessness of the beginning which deceives people about this form's cunning method of evil. Charity may become a pest, social care turn to tyranny, medical help to questionable tampering, enlightenment and information to levelling and stupefying, assistance to enslavement, political activity to brutality.

Alongside these forms of 'institutionalized evil' appearing coldly and impersonally in all possible arrangements and forms of society, 'individualized evil' also often appears in a strangely objective and cold form. The so-called desk murderers of Nazi Germany come to mind who, without engaging themselves or getting their hands dirty, signed orders for the murder of thousands. It can be observed more and more frequently, especially among juvenile criminals, that the motivation for their deeds is not to be sought in a strong passion but in sober calculation and seemingly colourless ideas and thoughts. As a juvenile criminal said: 'I just wanted to see what it's like to kill somebody'. Or one hears: 'Something in me made me do it'—as if a double could be pointed out who was responsible for the deed. At least it seems quite obvious that one must look more in the area of the non-personal evil for the motives of criminal offences. They no longer seem to be as much determined by emotions and drives as by thoughts and deliberations. With this, a change is announced which will be discussed later.

It belongs to the phenomena of institutionalized evil that in many places situations have arisen leading to insoluble problems. One only needs to say Berlin, Israel, Vietnam and everybody knows what is meant. Political, military, social and other situations of conflict have been created which cannot be healed in a peaceful manner. Whatever was done to clean up these potentially explosive areas, new injustices would inevitably arise.

How have these and other situations developed? It can hardly be assumed that the statesmen making the decisions were fully conscious of the consequences of their deeds. Granted that the most noble and humane intentions may not always have been present, it still seems absurd to accuse those statesmen of having intentionally implemented plans which would later have to be called despicable and deplorable. The examples rather show irresponsible actions taken without a total view of a situation in an unconscious, half-dreaming or otherwise shrouded condition of soul. Decisions originating from dark, suppressed states of consciousness are gateways for negative forces in both private and public life. Our century demands decisions taken with clear, all-human insight. If we allow negative forces the chance to be established, potential conflict and distress is created which in its resilience is hard to overcome. Regardless of exactly how these insoluble conflicts have come about, it can be stated as a fact that such potentially explosive situations largely escape human efforts to change them. The situations seem to take off on their own, reinforce themselves and as if by their own inertia keep rolling on. Human intervention often enough causes reactions which prompt new and increased conflicts. Simply: once created, the evil becomes an institution and then continues by itself.

One thing is certain: the twentieth century which accomplished undreamed of advances in the fields of technology and the natural sciences has not only made no progress in the moral sphere but is threatening to sink into moral barbarity. In order to reach a positive development here, it seems necessary first to come to a theoretical understanding of evil.

The Growth of Evil

It is often assumed that man remains the same throughout the ages, but particularly with reference to the existence of evil we can show how significant changes have occurred during his evolution. In reality the 'Fall' is not a completed occurrence but an on-going process with many stages. In the darkness of human beginnings a seed was planted whose growth can be observed in the course of history.

Persian mythology distinguishes two cosmic worlds: one of light and the other of darkness. Against the god of light, Ahura Mazdao, who is as high above the sun as the sun is above the earth, fights Ahriman, who has established his kingdom in the depths of the earth. Like two principles of nature, good and evil oppose each other. Day and night, light and darkness, are but other forms expressing good and evil and morality here is still considered synonymous with the cosmic. Good and evil sustain a well balanced relationship with each other, like sun and earth. Their balance is a problem of cosmic organization into which man is placed: the laws of nature and the laws of morality belong together. Thus man is inevitably involved in nature's rhythms and oscillations between these two cosmic powers, much like a flower or an animal. So one cannot yet speak of moral achievements in the sense of personal decisions. Much as a rose opens to the sunlight, man can let the cosmic light of the good enter him. He is not 'evil' in an individual sense, just as an animal led by its instincts cannot be considered evil. In the later forms of the Mithraic religion this basic oscillating dualism finds a third balancing principle in Mithras, the divine mediator, who helps man in the fight between Ahura Mazdao and Ahriman. This indicates the first appearance of a fragile element of moral decision. Cosmic forces immeasurably high above the human being and formerly opposed begin to approach and touch the periphery of his personality. There arises the demand for an individual choice between the two world principles.

Nordic mythology does not recognize a personal human Fall either. It is the Aesir, not man, who fall prey to evil! During a banquet, Loki, the Nordic Lucifer, derides the assembled gods: 'Do you, Odin, remember how we mixed our blood in ancient times?' At Loki's instigation the Aesir, during the construction of their castle, become guilty of fraud and breach of contract with the giants, because the giants were cheated out of their promised gold which Loki later stole. Since that time war and strife have prevailed in the world and the curse attached to the gold is passed on to man, even to Siegfried and the Nibelungs. The problem connected with all knowledge is touched on with this simile—as the Bible also indicates that all pre-Christian knowledge derives from Lucifer. ('But the serpent said to the woman, "You will not die. For God knows that when you eat it your eyes will be opened, and you will be like God, knowing good and evil".' Gen.3:4,5.) Germanic mythology expresses the conviction that ultimately evil is God's business into which man has been tragically drawn without being fully responsible: an infliction imposed upon the Aesir gods and passed on to man.

In Greek mythology Hephaestos shows certain traits of the Lucifer spirit. He is the ruler over fire, busying himself in the sooty forge, dirty, ugly and crude; he has thin legs and is lame, like the devil of the Middle Ages. He has been thrown out of heaven like Lucifer. In the picture of this limping god one can see a profound truth. Evil is all that cannot keep up with the development of the good. It limps behind in the divine world evolution. The Greek soul felt its love of harmony offended and called on the artistic sense to oppose Hephaestos. Evil is unlovely and ugly; it is embarrassing and is overcome by humour. It seems as if the Greek was either unable, or did not want, to recognize evil at its core—as if a veil is drawn to hide or lessen the terrible. Like Goethe, the Greek made evil appear ridiculous and comical so that he did not have to portray it in its tragic monstrosity, which he would not have been able to bear. This may seem a mere skimming of the depths, such as Nietzsche refers to in regard to Hellenic culture. One could also say the time had not yet come when evil could be faced for what it really is. To evaluate the mystery of evil on the basis of aesthetics expresses both an inability to go deeper into the problem and an urge for protection from its full power. The ugly limping Hephaestos causes the gods to laugh at him whenever he appears before them: 'Tremendous laughter was heard from the blessed gods when they saw Hephaestos busily moving about'. That evil to the Greek was a problem of aesthetics is emphasized by another strange twist of mythology: Hephaestos is married to Aphrodite, the goddess of love and *beauty*! The ugly-evil is the other side of beauty; they are most closely connected. Through this marriage of Hephaestos and Aphrodite it becomes evident that Greek mythology does not recognize an actual moral problem or experiences it as such. Evil is interpreted as ugly, it dirties and disturbs the divine harmony. It is partner and counterpart of the beautiful. Art strives for understanding of the riddle of evil, giving it a form appropriate to the experience of men at that time, and sublimating it through aesthetic portrayal.

Not until the Middle Ages is evil experienced as a personal question. The Persian saw it as part of a natural cosmic order, the Germanic tribes as a concern of the gods and the Greek as an artistic problem. Only in the Middle Ages does it completely touch man and become part of his inner self and therewith a matter of personal morality and individual suffering. During the centuries following the birth of Christ one can observe a process of involution as evil comes down from cosmic heights and takes up residence within man himself. Immense inner struggles have gripped the hearts of men from St. Augustine to Luther. Monks, nuns and knights fought the enemy within. They fasted, prayed and chastised themselves in order to overcome the adversary. The word covering all these struggles is 'asceticism'. The attempt was made to get a hold on that dangerous, seductive power by deadening and eliminating the lower instincts. The body with its needs and cravings, 'nature' as such was perceived as evil. 'Nature is sin.' By suppressing the natural, weakening the body, by destruction, avoidance and refusal, they tried to keep the seducer in check.

With the beginning of the age of natural sciences, discoveries and inventions, we enter a new period in the development of evil. The burdens and demands approaching man through the totally altered conditions of life cause him conflicts quite unknown in earlier times. The modern civilization which spread over a large part of the globe in less than a hundred years changed the structure of human existence. The natural protection of religion and social forms, supported by a framework of respected tradition, has disappeared. In place of rhythms of life determined by the quiet progression of nature, the laws of a new age are dictated by railway, automobile, aircraft, cinema, radio, TV, space exploration and computer technology. Advancing technology and automation have created entirely new professions. Industry and economy have become the decisive factors of existence. The struggle for existence is getting harder every year. The technical, political, national and other administrative machineries cover life with a dense network of laws, regulations and directions and intrude into the privacy of every individual. Life is more and more complicated, hurried and exhausting. Nobody for any length of time can escape these influences, approaching through a thousand channels. Not only city people but even farmers are being drawn into this whirlpool of civilization. Entirely new temptations, dangers and possibilities of deviation are arising in our time.

Since the boundaries are getting blurred, in countless matters it is becoming very difficult to distinguish between good and evil. Such a confusing mixture arises that one can no longer manage with a plain black-and-white technique. Insoluble conflicts of conscience, previously restricted to a few unusual life situations, are becoming a daily occurrence. In many countries millions of citizens are constantly torn between their own conscience and the demands of dictatorial leadership. The inner conflicts of the freedom fighters who, especially in Nazi Germany during World War II, had to decide between their love of country and their duty to resist the evident injustices, were unbelievably hard. Many situations arise in professional or business life where it is exceedingly difficult to behave in such a way as to stay upright between light and darkness, justice and injustice. In political life, in economic activity connected with institutions of state and government, conditions have become such that just because of the complexity of everything involved, it is ever more difficult if not impossible for participants to conduct themselves perfectly correctly. In many situations one simply does not know any longer how to manage without lies, fraud and deception. It would be unrealistic to deny that in many cases white lies, for example, are almost unavoidable. Without recourse to such means, in dealing with their government in countries led by dictatorships, millions of people would daily risk their freedom, the safety of their relatives and even their own lives. Dilemmas such as these have always existed (religious casuistry abounds with examples) but at no other time in history has their volume and range expanded to such a degree. Whole nations and continents are covered by a network of extorted lies, from which there seems to be no escape. We see evil, in seemingly irresistible waves of attack, approaching man, grasping him and permeating him from within. Disquietingly, inevitably, he finds himself drawn into entanglement and guilt. Evil does not only operate more directly and intensively, it begins to lay hold of additional areas of human nature. Before our modern times it appeared predominantly in the soul realm; now it also penetrates the spiritual realm of man. In the past the soul was attacked by tempting forces which yet permitted the core of personality to remain untouched and complete. Now, increasingly, temptation seems to lead to a penetration of the entire being, including thinking and the centre of personality. Therefore it has now become necessary to fight as a fully conscious individual whereas formerly it was still sufficient to distinguish good and evil by feeling. How little that suffices in the present and how undermined the sense of moral discrimination has already become is shown by the experiences of this century. The mystery of evil is becoming the cardinal question from which nobody can escape for long, even if he may still be relatively protected. We are standing before the great unveiling of the mystery of evil which is connected with the mystery of true humanity: for true humanity can only be fully achieved after the tempter's great trials have been successfully encountered.

Contemporary man cannot and must not avoid confrontation with the tempter unless he would forgo the opportunity of reaching a higher human level. As evil has come closer and closer to man, no longer a cosmic power far away, and has become a force active in his own being, it is now placed within the range of human responsibility. Through collision with antagonistic forces men are called upon to develop higher powers of good within themselves. Through obstacles they are to become stronger and experience inner growth. By meeting evil they can gain maturity and wisdom. It serves no purpose to cry over a lost paradisal innocence and an existence weighed down by sin and guilt. Since the Fall, this is established fact. The question can only be how we can overcome its consequences. The important thing is no longer to preserve innocence and purity of soul—these have been lost long ago and have to be regained in different ways. This is expressed by the Parsifal legend where we are told that the young Parsifal as 'Pure Fool' cannot find entrance to the castle of the Holy Grail. Only after he has gone through earthly misery and guilt and has learned to understand through compassion, do the gates of the castle open for him. This does not mean that we should take guilt lightly—as the over-subtle intellect might infer—nor that we should even wish for it so as to gain earthly maturity. Christ taught us to pray, 'And lead us not into temptation, but deliver us from evil' (Matt.6:13)—thereby putting one of the deepest concerns of the human soul into prayer, since the man who really understands himself will always feel fear under the assault of evil world powers and will seek redemption. By speaking this prayer, however, Christ pointed out very clearly that evil exists in the world and that we have to struggle with it. As the child during his first attempts at standing and walking has to fall and stub his toe before he can stand and walk freely, so men must fall into guilt and sin and be bruised on the hard facts of evil to gain higher abilities thereby. We may not wish for such painful experiences either for ourselves or for others, but equally we cannot be spared them. 'The soul should never wish to fall, but must gain wisdom from the fall.'* It is not enough to avoid evil and keep away from it. It is not to be fought from outside but to be changed from within. With this the deep meaning of Christ's words, as yet not fully explored, begins to be revealed. 'But I say to you, Do not resist one who is evil. But if any one strikes you on the right cheek, turn to him the other also' (Matt.5:39). It is part of the endless mystery of evil that it has to be present in order to increase the good. As a deadly poison from the physician's hand may heal, so from the hand of the divine world-physician, the poison of evil is present ultimately for our salvation. We must make sure that we do not meet its influences passively! By increasing our efforts to overcome it we may wrest from it the strength for which purpose it has been imposed upon us in the first place. When it receives a poisonous medicine, the organism *unconsciously* summons the powers of resistance the physician desires: when we meet evil, we have to resist it *consciously*. In this sense one may speak of a transformation of evil, an idea to which an old Indian saying points: 'As Shiva does with poison, so the nobleman with the mistakes of others: he does not spit them out of his mouth, he does not take them into his heart, no, he digests them.'

In a Christian sense the poison is not restricted to what is inflicted from without: one's own malignity has also to be 'digested', changed and transformed. R. M. Rilke expressed this thought of evil's transformation in one of his letters: 'We should be able to forget about those old myths which are transmitted from the origins of all peoples; the myths of the dragons which at the last moment are transformed into princesses; perhaps all the dragons of our life are princesses, only waiting to see us, for once, beautiful and brave. Perhaps everything terrible is, essentially, that which is helpless, and asking our help.'

* Steiner, *The Souls' Awakening*, vi. Steiner Book Centre, Toronto, 1973.

The Growth of Evil

These examples show a progressive approach and gradual evolution of evil. Thus each period of development has received its special task which has to be resolved.

Persian cosmology:	Evil is a part of cosmic orders and tensions into which man is planted.
European mythology:	Evil is the tragic guilt of the gods and man is drawn into it.
Greece:	Evil is an influx of the repulsive, disturbing the harmony of the world; it can be overcome by art.
Middle Ages:	Evil is a matter of the soul's personal morality and has to be destroyed through asceticism.
Our own time:	Evil must be transformed and effect a strengthening of the good by calling forth powers of resistance.

The gradual evolution of evil can be seen in the development of the 'Faust idea' in a different way and in a different perspective. A forerunner of Faust, possibly the first known, is Job. His precedence is not only interesting from a literary point of view, since Goethe received from it important stimulation for his *Faust*, but much more; it draws our immediate sympathy as one of the most outstanding examples of this idea of man.

The Book of Job in the Old Testament does not belong to the dusty or outdated documents of time long past; it is rather one of the most fascinating books of world literature and in a certain sense is still very modern. It is remarkable in having been written almost in the form of a drama which could be put on the stage without major alterations. Its presentation, sprinkled with brief commentaries like stage directions, proceeds almost exclusively in direct speech. One may assume that it was meant as some kind of cult drama of the Old Testament, comparable to the mystery dramas of antiquity. The prelude to the First Act leads the observer into spiritual realms and lets him see the spiritual-divine background of human fate. It is the 'Prologue in Heaven,' during which God the Father among the 'Sons of God', the Angels, gives Satan a clearly defined liberty to interfere with Job's fate. From this liberty, expressed in detail, which man's adversary received from God, there resulted the plagues, difficulties and blows which Job experienced. He himself does not know anything of the adversary's mission and his innocent trust in God remains at first undaunted and strong: 'Shall we received good at the hand of God, and shall we not receive evil?' (Job 2:10). Not until the discussions with his three friends, who arrive as the voices of yesterday and, as representatives of devout orthodox tradition, demand in their rigid, righteous ways blind faith alone, does Job come to ask about the purpose of his suffering. 'Let me know why thou dost contend against me.' (Job 10:2.) For the first time the question of understanding is being posed, which is immeasurably stronger than belief. To the horror of his friends Job dares to cry out: 'And even if it be true that I have erred, my error remains with myself.' (Job 19:4). In a grandiose development Job step by step grows self-conscious and independent and finally, with Faustian-Promethean self-assertion, he dares God to explain. And the astonishing thing happens; God actually meets the challenge of this little human individuality who, courageous in his yearning for understanding, expects the answer to the riddle of his life. God angrily condemns the three old men as poor administrators of his will, although in the sense of traditional faith they spoke 'piously' enough. He approves the fourth friend who arrived later and who, as one of the young, was not tarnished by outmoded tradition, but represented that impulse of mankind based on the individual personality, which is also alive

The Growth of Evil

in Job. In the dramatic composition, the Godhead thereby acknowledges the Faustian effort of the human ego that is seeking to understand. Certain representatives of orthodox faiths in our day, who cannot sufficiently condemn the Faustian struggle for understanding as blasphemy, would be well advised to re-read this particular sanctioning by God of the awakening thinking force, as written in the Book of Job. Like the three incorrigible old friends they only repeat again and again: 'For inquire, I pray you, of bygone ages, and consider what the fathers have found; for we are but of yesterday, and know nothing . . .' (Job 8:8–9).

The Book of Job conveys the meaningful answer from God to the suffering seeker of knowledge which gives him an insight beyond religious tradition into the characteristics of evil and its role in the interplay of guilt and penitence. The mysterious picture of Behemoth and Leviathan presents in picture form the only thing which can make sense at the height of the drama: the unveiling of the part the adversary has played in Job's fate. Job receives an explanation of the function of those forces which God allows to hinder natural development so that man may wring the good from them, and hence experience a strengthening of his abilities which would otherwise remain weak and dependent. An important part of the riddle of Job's fate is answered by his pain. His striving is acknowledged and he can say to God: 'I have heard of thee by the hearing of the ear, but now my eye sees thee' (Job 42:5).

In God's instruction concerning Leviathan, a deeply mysterious word is written which like lightning illumines future possibilities. The voice of God asks, 'Will he make a covenant with you to take him for your servant for ever?' (Job 41:4.) Thus for the first time in history was the 'pact with the devil' spoken of. God himself placed this vision of immeasurable possibilities before Job. However, the time had not yet come: Job was allowed only a brief glance into the mysterious background of destiny where, hidden from human sight at first, the world of evil is secretly woven. It was not yet the hour for evil to stand face to face with man.

The 'pact with the devil' which implies a more or less conscious, willing invocation of negative forces was not at that time in the realm of the human will. It is very revealing that this part of the Faust motif appears in an early Christian legend, from an age when the enormous transition of consciousness from antiquity to modern times was beginning. In those days the last spiritual abilities of the soul which had their roots in heathen mysteries were waning, making way for thinking, which began to awaken through observation of nature. With this step towards intellectualization of thought there came a new relationship with evil. The development of the 'pact' is symptomatic of the changed situation. Legend permits Cyprian, the sorcerer, who endeavoured to win the love of the virgin Justina, to make a pact with evil spirits. However, as they could not harm Justina who was leading a holy life, Cyprian ended his pact with evil and became Christian. Obviously the 'Faust' here is represented only by his daring attempt to make the pact, for the motive of his deed has nothing in common with the Faustian urge to understand.

The Theophilus legend of later origin is similar. Theophilus, head of a diocese, is relieved of his duties, enters into covenant with the devil and is thereupon reinstated. Suffering strong pangs of conscience, he asks the Virgin Mary for help and she gives him back an incriminating page bearing his signature. The chance to make use of the adversary's powers which was offered to Job shows up only lightly in the Cyprian and Theophilus legends. The appearance of the new versions of the pact indicates that these legends were widely known during the Middle Ages. The great and far-reaching response showed that they meant something to the general consciousness of those times.

A further step in the evolution of the Faust idea, which was slowly being born from the depths of the soul, was the appearance of the legend that gave it a name. The tale of Dr. Johannes Faustus, as well as the folk play and the puppet play derived from it, enjoyed a most enthusiastic reception from all classes of people throughout central Europe during the seventeenth and eighteenth centuries. People felt that something basically human was involved there that nobody could avoid. Regardless of how colourful the individual components of the legend may be, one can see clearly how the main motif emerges from the mass of subordinate detail—the Faustian quest for understanding. It is very moving to read what kind of questions Faust asks the devil. He asks about the secrets of the stars, the nature of paradise, even about the nature of the angels. The sixteenth century had come to the point where man found it necessary to ask the devil about the angels! Religious traditions could give him no satisfactory insight into the nature of the spiritual world, but brushed him off with pious dogma, insufficient for his thinking. This left him no choice but to turn to those forces which up to then had been taboo. He calls up the adversary because he cannot suppress his inner yearning for understanding and needs an answer to the riddles of life, regardless of cost. This is the situation of modern man who undertakes the dangerous task of knocking at the door of forces below the threshold of humanity, impelled by a longing for knowledge given him by God. The atomic scientist is the Faust of today. He enters into a pact with the spiritual forces behind matter, unaware that with the signature in blood he is pawning himself and mankind. Is not that exactly the extent of the hubris of which Faust is accused and which of necessity has to end in hell? The Faust of legend ends up as a condemned man. Must that be the fate of those who, like him, are challenging the dark forces?

That the *accusatus et damnatus* (accused and damned) of the puppet play cannot be the last word on Faust was felt for the first time by Lessing. He projected a drama to depict the redemption of the guilty Faust.

Goethe carried the thought of Faust's redemption to its highest point and thereby opened a new chapter in the evolution of the Faust idea. His artistic version allows for the truth that, in spite of all, it is not presumption and hubris if Faustian man enters the risky contract with the spirits of temptation, but a necessary fate—a last consequence of the original Fall which, as pointed out in connection with Job, is allowed by God to be included in his plan of education. Through the event that took place on Golgotha, man can find the strength to enable him to overcome the Fall into sin and error and be led upward again. Goethe felt very clearly that redemption does not mean only the erasure of guilt: the 'minus' resulting from guilt is not merely balanced by an equally large 'plus'—rather the minus is to be changed into a plus so that every debt of guilt may become a respective sum of good. Through Christ, the Fall is brought to fruition in an increase of good. Grace, helping from above, annuls Faust's guilt and helps him to change his faults and weaknesses into virtues and abilities. The immortal part of his soul, now qualified as a member of the higher worlds through his experiences, is taken by divine spiritual forces into their service.

Faust becomes the teacher of children who died very young, because he did not pass in vain through all the depths and abysses of the earth but gained experience, maturity and wisdom, which those who pass away very young do not have. Thus guilt leads him to light through suffering. The Faust idea reaches a new stage with the incorporation of the Christ impulse. Job could only vaguely feel and hope: 'For I know that my Redeemer lives'. (Job 19:25.) In Goethe's *Faust* that prophecy comes true.

The Growth of Evil

In the history of the Faust idea, we see how evil reaches increasingly deeply into man's developing life and consciousness. With Job it appears as a force allowed by God, at first unrecognized and behind the scenes of outer happenings. Although it is already there, only through a dream-like, mystical image does man sense it as if in anticipation in the words about the pact with the devil. Cyprian and Theophilus mark two intermediate steps: while the covenant with evil is made for a period of time the motivation for it must be seen in primitive passionate aberrations. The legendary Dr. Faustus already showed a modern scientific man who does not call up the devil because of passion running wild, but because of his yearning for understanding. However, he falls prey to the adversary. Finally Goethe's Faust is the erring but forever striving man who can be redeemed.

Evil — the Touchstone
for Freedom

We have shown how the twentieth century has brought an increase of evil which one would not have dared to foresee at its beginning. It is strange how suddenly this phenomenon appears. Even though the First World War, as apocalyptic prelude, unleashed terrible events, the real drama of evil did not come until later, almost exactly at the end of the first third of the century. The year 1933, during which National Socialism took over government in Germany, is the year of the incipient unveiling of evil. Some day perhaps, this moment will be counted among the secret crossing points of history when important happenings took place behind the scenes of the readily observable. Mankind entered a new stage in its painful relationship to evil. Up till then evil mostly avoided broad daylight—from then onwards it appeared with a recklessness and shamelessness previously unknown.

In view of these and other facts only touched on here, there is a question in many hearts as to the meaning of what is happening. It is often asked bitterly and desperately: 'Is there no kind of justice?' Or in religious terms: 'How can God allow this?' The agony behind such a question will not be removed by a few quick replies. One has to have experienced it and suffered it before one can hope to come closer to solving it. Many attempts have been made to answer the riddle of how divine love can be compatible with the unbelievable power of evil on earth. Among these deliberations there is an answer which, apart from satisfying the intellect, is capable of standing up to the realities of life and gives strength to master them: *God permits the evolution of evil for the sake of human freedom.* .

It can be observed that evil evolves in the same measure as the principle of freedom begins to be realized. A free being must have unrestricted possibilities of choice. A man must be able to decide for or against God on his own—freedom cannot otherwise be conceived. It would be a contradiction to call it that without admitting at least two principles to choose from. The argument that since God is almighty he could have given the gift of freedom unaccompanied by the risk of erring cannot be allowed. This would be non-sensical—like demanding a triangle with two sides. Freedom without choice is equally meaningless. Hence the Godhead, not only formally but in all reality, has admitted a counter-principle so that man can freely decide between the two possibilities.

This human freedom has not come about suddenly and it is not absolute. Rather, it has grown very gradually during long processes of evolution, appearing in limited measure at first. Men are neither free nor unfree—they are on the path to freedom. With laborious effort one small measure after another is gained, a task which not even God can do for them if it is not to be a superficial freedom. As with all evolution, long periods when nothing seems to happen alternate with times when it advances almost suddenly and with a leap.

At each new step of freedom gained the Godhead releases man from his guidance in an appropriate degree. With the growing range of freedom there is necessarily combined an increase in danger and responsibility. The tasks done by God for man during the preceding stages now have to be done by man himself and lead to an increased contact and conflict with those powers whose existence is to give freedom its full value. Only that which maintains itself in face of the adversary has passed the golden test. This may be compared to a child's stages of development. At first he cannot do anything for himself, his parents have to nurture his early growth and guide his steps for quite some time. Gradually the parents step back and the independent personality of the young individual awakens more and more. A period of quasi-freedom has to be lived through—as with mankind as a whole—until the grown-up person can take on his own responsibilities. Notwithstanding their love the parents must not spare the child his own experiences. Up to a point temptations and mistakes have to be risked and suffered. The only difference in the 'education of mankind' towards independence is that much greater temptations and dangers are admitted, in keeping with the much larger aim. If one wished to spare mankind these heavier trials, one would be wishing that men should not rise beyond their present degree of development.

The twentieth century, so emphatically revealed as very special, is bringing a new widening of the area of freedom and with this a new and additional confrontation with evil. They are irrevocably connected. By the degree of the one, we may infer the magnitude of the other. Thus we actually see how man enters realms formerly closed to him, how he stakes his claim there by widening the measure of freedom and responsibility and how on the other hand he is being grasped by the forces of darkness and feverishly shaken. Among the numerous phenomena of this kind none more clearly demonstrates what has been said than the discovery of atomic energy: with unbelievable expansion of human freedom on the one hand and equally gigantic temptations on the other. While previous discoveries and innovations were given to man in the natural course of development, with atomic energy he has entered an area which, to quote a modern scientist, has hitherto been reserved for God alone:

the inner structure of matter and the energy residing in it. Friedrich von Weizsäcker speaks of transgressing the boundaries and conditions of the original natural existence and continues: 'Speaking in terms of antiquity he [man] is entering a realm in which there are no gods, or whose gods are foreign to us'.* One may well fear the dimension of the abyss opened by the possible misuse of atomic energy, and now perilously close, but one should also recognize that the responsibility thus created is the expression of a new increase in freedom. Speaking in human terms, the Godhead must trust that the created being will be able to handle the task given to him and that he will be conscious of the honour thus bestowed on him. There is a similar prospect of untold possibilities arising out of research in modern biology, such as the experimental manipulations of chromosomal structures aiming at accomplishing artificial mutations and creating a totally new man. The threat here is of interference in the moral, soul and spiritual foundations of human life, leading possibly to its irreversible deterioration. The grandiose successes of space exploration have also very much enlarged the sphere of freedom. Here too exists a conceivable misuse for military purposes but for the sake of an increase in human faculties, the danger must be run.

For these reasons we cannot whole-heartedly affirm the ever-present complaint about increasing evil. Evil must be seen as the other side of positive facts. Depressing as is the opening of the abyss, it does not only mean deliverance to dark forces—it may cause the awakening of other forces which up to now have been active from outside and beyond freedom. Each new danger brings with it an increase in man's strength of soul. Each new temptation is a challenge.

* *The World View of Physics*, Routledge and Kegan Paul, London, 1952.

The Two Faces of Evil

However manifold are the opinions regarding the role played by evil in the world and man, they all agree in their emphasis on the *polarity of good and evil*. But what is gained by this statement—is it not taken for granted that good and evil are polar opposites? Certainly it would be absurd not to recognize the difference between them; and yet the mere opposition of one to the other harbours a danger and is liable to hide the actual facts or make them appear slanted and incomplete. The tensions which occur and which we conveniently blame on the dichotomy of good and evil have different contexts and are much more complicated than at first appears.

To show what is meant we shall list a number of bad or imperfect and undesirable traits, predispositions and tendencies, so that through these the tensions may be studied. From the array of phenomena which may be classified as evil, or at least negative, we select these qualities: miserliness, arrogance, pedantry, cowardice, vacillation, indifference, ambition, effusiveness. For each of these we shall try to find the appropriate positive or good trait. If we wanted to do this simply by looking for the opposite quality we could say something like: the opposite of miserliness is squandering . . . no, it is thriftiness. We may be perplexed already by these two antonyms we have found. Let us take a few additional examples. Arrogance; as opposite we find either underestimation of self—or self-confidence. Pedantry—disorderliness, and orderliness. Cowardice; recklessness—and bravery. These few attempts have put us on the right track: each of the negative traits listed has two 'opposites', one on the negative side and one on the positive—the latter also standing in polar relation to the second negative element. We can set out a list as follows:

miserliness	thriftiness	wastefulness
arrogance	self-confidence	lack of self-confidence
pedantry	orderliness	disorderliness
cowardice	bravery	recklessness
vacillation	equanimity	rigidity
apathy	interest	over-susceptibility
ambition	perseverance	indolence
effusiveness	compassion	coldness

From this table, which could be further expanded, an important law becomes evident. In each area of inner life there are *two* kinds or directions of evil. Evil can enter human souls by two gateways.

Among the phenomena of evil, opposites and counterparts come to light, confronting each other in pairs. The good in each case is to be found between the extremes, not only balancing but raising and transforming them. The polar forces of evil would only cancel each other out. If one imagines two such forces of evil active in one person and of equal strength, then if nothing else happened the two tendencies would annul each other. Imagine someone who in a given situation feels both fear and foolhardiness. If he did not take a decisive step in this counterplay of forces, no solution would emerge. Bravery does arise from a mixture of fear and foolhardiness, but because man's own will moves, conquering and transforming the two opposing forces. In each case good is the outcome when a struggle between two polar forces is decided by the employment of the human will.

Now we can see why it is misleading to consider only the tension between good and evil. In a sense, the good is not the real opposite of evil, because this whole problem is not one of duality but trinity. There are *three* characteristics in the balance. Evil is split within itself and by itself forms a duality. Thus to make clear the relationship between good and evil, we must not think in terms of opposites such as upper and lower, right and left, but must visualize the whole as a trinity. Evil itself is split into a 'right' and a 'left'. The good, however, is the centre standing above both, which separates the two forces from their barren opposition and lifts them to a higher plane. The good is not simply the point of balance between two evil extremes but the higher unity within which one-sided forces are made useful for something better. In it, the two forces leading to evil find a form of redemption.

Now we take a further step. Let us look once more at the table on page 37. Is it just by chance that for each example we have one good and two bad traits? Is it possible to recognize a definite concurrence in the two deviating tendencies? Quite generally one could say that one side in the soul leads to over-indulgence, over-emphasis, form-lessness, dissipation, over-exuberance (there are three words here with the prefix 'over'). The other danger leads to a kind of diminishing, to densification, hardening, stagna-tion; and these are paralysing, deadening tendencies. While the one deviation has the effect of a centrifugal soul-spiritual force, the other acts centripetally. According to our table the following traits belong together.

On the one side:	*On the other side:*
recklessness	cowardice
arrogance	lack of self-confidence
vacillation	rigidity
disorderliness	pedantry

The Two Faces of Evil

over-susceptibility	apathy
wastefulness	miserliness
ambition	indolence
effusiveness	coldness

In these contrasts we find something typical, but we still lack the real yardstick for measurement. It is given to us when we consider man's relation to the earth! It is here we have to look for the pivot on which this problem turns. Man has been born into this world but his origin is in spiritual realms which are not 'of this world' and he returns to them after death. His task in life consists in impressing the stamp of that higher world, to which he is most deeply indebted, upon this world on earth. In other words he fulfils his earthly task only if, within earth-existence, he brings the spirit to manifestation. There are two main possibilities of error: to fall prey to the material laws of the earth and forsake the spiritual task; or to fail to find a proper relation to the earth and its necessities and 'hover above the earth' without accomplishing one's earthly task. *Craving for the earth*, and *flight from the earth* are the two errors of life to which man may fall victim.

These are the two common denominators to which we may reduce the many forms of guilt and mistake. Here we have the measure for the manifestations of evil in their dual nature. The right side of our table opposite contains some particular forms of *over-estimation of the earthly*, the left, symptoms of *under-estimation of the earthly*. The tendencies on the one side are disguised forms of *craving for the earth*, those on the other more or less camouflaged forms of *flight from the earth*.

The above examples concern opposite pairs of 'evil' qualities which show an obvious relation to corresponding 'good' qualities. We have now gained the background which will enable us to analyse correctly other phenomena of evil where it is not so easy to see the negative extremes relating to one higher element of the good. We know there are many offences, bad habits and aberrations for which it may be difficult, if not impossible, to find a directly opposed form of evil. But this is not really all that important. It is more important to understand that there are observable in the human soul forms of evil that are opposed to each other. We have characterized this polarity as follows: Everything that leads to over-estimation of the earthly, all camouflaged craving for it, is the one side of evil; this is opposed by the other extreme which reveals itself as an erroneous under-estimation of the earthly, going as far as desire to escape from it altogether. Over-estimation and craving for this earth are followed by hardening, ossification, cramp, estrangement from the spiritual, stagnation, paralysis and death. Under-estimation and escape from what is of the earth are accompanied by disintegration, intoxication, illusion, loss of form and insanity.

This duality of evil is closely connected with man's own nature. Body, soul and spirit are its three components. The soul shares the life of the body on the one hand and receives from the body through the sense organs the impressions of the earthly plane. Thus the soul partakes of the physical world and the physical world gives it impressions in many different ways. On the other hand the soul also opens itself to the spirit. A world that is higher and independent of the physical presents itself and allows the soul to partake of the divine. Swinging between the spiritual world and the physical world, the soul finds the right harmony between these poles if it can inwardly manage to permeate with spirit all it experiences on the earth and at the same time can let the rays of the spirit shine down into earthly activity. This dual achievement constitutes the healing balance and the higher unity for the two tendencies of human life which, left to themselves, lead to evil.

The Two Faces of Evil

The two forces of evil strive to hold the pendulum to the one or the other side as it is swinging. The one tempter's goal is to fasten a man's attention entirely upon his necessary preoccupation with earthly matters and to keep him from illumining the earth with the light of spirit. He is to become totally bound to material existence and in this bondage to forget his spiritual origin. The other tempter seeks the opposite, wishing to fill the soul with the urge towards a self-sufficient, exclusively spiritual life. This force gives the soul a desire to be detached from earthly duties and responsibilities, to live in an egotistical yearning for bliss hearing nothing of earthly troubles and tasks. A man's severance from the spiritual and bondage to the material is the goal of the one tempter: his separation from earthly existence and lapse into a nebulous, unrealistic spirituality, antagonistic to earth, is the aim of the other seducer. The first would drag him down to the level of an animal-man, content with the dull satisfaction of physical needs: the latter would make him the caricature of an angel, unfaithful to earth in egotistical arrogance, conceit and self-deification.

It can be seen that good and evil are actually not in a simple polar opposition; but how often are not moral judgments made on the basis of such an opposition! Something is recognized as evil and its opposite considered good, without any suspicion that this opposite is often only another evil. This is why it is so important to get away from the simple dualism, 'good and evil' and recognize a threefold structure.

The opposite forms of evil tend to balance each other. This occurs naturally and means that the counterplay of the two escapes notice and the effect remains negative. Men must learn to perceive the counterplay of the two tempters and consciously, by inner effort, produce a balance. For if nothing bad is being created, nothing good is happening either and in reality we have stagnation and regression. As the tension between positive and negative electricity is used to produce power or light, so in the soul the tension of the two poles of evil should be guided to produce a spiritual force yielding light or life. Without a conscious striving the dangers can alternate, now degrading a man to the animalistic, then bemusing him with an inner life disturbed by illusion. Such conditions can be observed in the making.

In modern life attention is often absorbed during the day by purely mundane, technical or economic matters serving only the maintenance of the physical body and estranging people from the spiritual. Criticism is not intended, merely a statement of fact: it would be foolish not to face the demands of modern conditions. Yet, although permeation of life by spiritual forces is necessary, the pendulum often swings only towards intoxicating, stupefying entertainments and relaxations. One may think of the warning words in the Gospel of Luke: 'But take heed to yourselves lest your hearts be weighed down with dissipation and drunkenness and cares of this life'. (21:34).

Intoxication and worry about food belong to the relatively harmless physical level of life and are therefore mild examples of the real dangers of flight from the earth and enslavement to the earth. It is characteristic today that so many people, especially the young, try to overcome our materialism by seizing on drugs such as LSD, mescalin, marihuana and opium. They induce conditions of soul intoxication to escape the senselessness of existence and in doing so fall prey to the principle leading to escape from the earth. Sometimes the appearance of the two powers in daily life is very difficult to recognize and often occurs in a most complicated manner. So far we have only wished to indicate the general directions and the principal differences between them. However, with awareness of the dual nature of evil one becomes more and more able to perceive which side is involved in any specific case. It grows obvious that this dual nature is playing a much larger part in life than was supposed. The forces do not of course work in such a way that those pulling towards the earth are always active from the physical side and the others always from the soul-spiritual side. Both may be active within the spiritual, the soul or the physical part of man, and they then appear according to the respective characteristics of each of man's three members.

What lives in the soul as surging emotion and passion belongs in general to that seducer who would draw man away from this earth: the mood of soul which feels that earthly matters are beneath it, or are contaminating or subordinate. One knows the familiar other-worldliness that is fully happy only in contemplating concerns of the soul. Self-indulgence in feeling may be gratifying but is barren for life and lifts man ever further into illusions and fantastic regions of thought and feeling—as we see among men who imagine themselves world benefactors or become religious fanatics or ascetics who scorn this world. Other tendencies that have a troublesome life in the heads of men are sultry mysticism, hazy occultism and arrogant pseudo-spirituality. All these tendencies to disintegration and formlessness lead to misconception or falsification of reality and destroy respect for what is justified and necessary in the earthly; they propel those whom they possess into a spectral, shadowy 'higher' world populated and nourished by the countless illusions and absurdities of mankind.

The power that brings petrification is very different. Its field of activity can be found mainly in the application of a cold, earthbound intellect. All intellectual dealing with matter carries the danger of becoming barren and void of spirit. The soul dries up through working with rigid laws and lifeless formulae. It is cut off from its source in a world of abstractions or empty formalism; and even the most brilliant intellectual ability cannot enliven the tundra of cold law and formula. Forces of death gain the upper hand over the soul—matter triumphs over spirit.

It is clear that scientific striving is particularly exposed to this danger, while artistic efforts are much closer to the other deviations of wild raving, illusion, and a deceptive dream-world. The dangers cannot be avoided, indeed must not be avoided, but must be recognized and overcome.

With the advance of intellectual knowledge and ability in technical matters, the spirit of the machine reigns widely over life today and reaps one triumph after another, making earth and man devoid of spirit. Stereotyping and technical levelling stunt creativity. Technology and intellectualism are both necessary, even irreplaceably important for our time, and only fools and dreamers can project a world without them. But now a desolation of soul, the spiritual insensitivity and enslavement of men to matter are calling up immeasurable catastrophe; and this is not the fault of technology, but of men. They do not wake the spiritual counterforces which could bring about a healthy balance. In time past, the danger of illusive estrangement was greater than that of earthly heaviness. In the present, earthly heaviness, constantly reinforced through intellectualism and technology, has become the danger.

In the Middle Ages, men had to wrestle more with superstition, magic, witchcraft, false mysticism, religious dreaming and decadent remnants of atavistic spiritual experience; these were the reefs on which many were stranded. The tendency to haziness and flight from the earth is not active in the same measure today. Now the danger is that people succumb to the onslaught of the spirit of earth's weight and the soul's death. As in a battle where the enemy attacks alternately on one wing and the other, the history of mankind in its struggle with the adversary shows it at one period exposed to the forces that darken the earth and at another to those that confuse the spirit and estrange men from the earth.

The good lies in the middle. Where the two extremes of evil are mastered, a man can rise beyond them. This means a permeation of the earthly with spirit and a deliberate guiding and forming of the soul. This middle position is not to be confused with any mass mediocity and indifference, or fear of decision and responsibility. The *aurea mediocritas*, the golden mean, has nothing to do with the desire never to get into a tight spot!

We degrade the good by opposing it to evil as a counterpart and contradiction. The good is in itself so perfect that it has no 'enemy'. It does not oppose, it redeems: it does not fight, it heals. The good as such makes no vital distinction between what is weakness and what is evil, but lovingly and transformingly redeems both.

Now that we have obtained an idea of the one-sided temptations within the human soul, it is not going to be too difficult to understand that the effects in the soul of the one or the other erroneous tendency can be found in the physical body. Body and soul are so closely intertwined that inevitably damage to the one eventually affects the other. With this in mind it may be permitted to look for the forces of evil in the bodily existence of man also. We need not superstitiously imagine the activity of the adversary in a crudely materialistic way and mumble about demons and physical devils taking hold of a human body. The body-soul-spirit structure of man has unity during his earthly life and because they inter-penetrate so closely, the evil force, which has to be envisaged as a purely spiritual entity, may manifest in each individual member. If this is understood it need not seem strange to look for the effects of evil in the physical body.

All processes in the physical body which lead to deposits and hardening, all sclerotic and calcifying processes are the tendencies begun in the soul by the petrifying force. A one-sided preoccupation over many years with dry intellectual activities may lead to sclerotic deposits in the body. People who are pedantic, small-minded, inflexible, unimaginative—ruled in fact by the head—are more prone to such illnesses as sclerosis and rheumatism than those who are young at heart, artistically mobile and vivacious. (Of course one must not conclude that such illnesses are always caused by particular attitudes of soul; they may quite well have other causes, possibly in the social environment.) Intellect, turned one-sidedly to earth, ages both soul and body. In fairy tales, the head's cold thinking is pictured as an aged crone who sits in a tower and spins. The young girl, taking the spindle, pricks her finger and falls as if dead.

All that makes the body age, that hardens it and causes illness through deposits, is caused by the world-calcifier, Death. In contrast all bodily processes which devour and dissolve, above all the phenomenon of fever, are the deeds of the power that tries to seduce man from the earth. Emotion, intoxication, ecstasy and illusion in the soul have their bodily counterpart in fever. Many a physician knows these correlations in certain illnesses.

We may also mention how the two forces of deviation appear with surprising clarity in certain mental illnesses. Schizophrenia, for example, in which consciousness is split and the wholeness of the personality is pulled apart, reveals the frightening archetype of the danger to which even a healthy man may succumb; only with him it is latent and does not manifest as strongly. In this illness, thinking, feeling and willing, which are normally in balanced interaction, become autonomous and no appropriate co-ordination of the three soul functions takes place. Thinking is not held in check by willing and, isolated from the realities of life, runs round in a labyrinth of self-spun fancies. It can seem rational, but is actually unrealistic and machine-like, under the spell of the cold intellectual power of darkness and mechanization. Willing on the other hand begins to operate instinctively, dominated by blunted feelings. The acts of will are not under the control of the personality but are done as if from a state of dreaming or drunkenness. Feeling is tossed between the extremes, alternating in triumphant arrogance and hollow self-effacement.

In the spiritual part of man also, these polarities appear. A comparison of religious outlooks may show the changing deviations. Arthur Drews for example, and many others, have seen in Christ only a mythological figure. Christ they say, was not a historical personality, but a personification of certain high ideals or of cosmic events. A contrary opinion sees him just as a great human being who founded a new religion by example and teachings. But Christ was neither a mythological figure, nor just a man. He was indeed a historical personality who lived on earth in a human body—but he was also more than human: in his human body lived the lofty divine being, the Logos itself. The tempter Lucifer, the deceiver about the realities of this earth who diverts man's gaze to aims beyond it, lives in the view of Christ as myth. The other view, acknowledging Christ as man only, is expressed by the spirit of earth-gravity who would separate humanity from the divine and, as in this case, prevent him from perceiving it in the earthly realm.

From what has already been said, it may be gathered that the reaction to the two tempting forces is rather different in man and in woman. Generally it is to be observed that men more than women are subject to the spirit of earthly weight and hardening. This can be seen in their more strongly earthbound intellectualism which, indeed, has brought about the technical era. Women on the other hand usually tend more towards dangers arising from an unmastered and uncontrolled soul life. Most of the religious ecstatics and dreamers of the Middle Ages were women. For this reason the Bible, in a most meaningful way, lets the tempter approach the woman: it is Eve who yields to the Serpent's whisper. This is the beautiful tempter into delusion and superficiality known to Christendom as Lucifer. In more modern times, with the dawning of natural science and technology, a new mythology arises in the story of Faust. Here it is the spirit of hardening and gravity who approaches the man as tempter. Mephistopheles turns to Faust and enters the pact with him. Although the figure of Mephistopholes is not quite consistently drawn, the spirit of earthly heaviness predominates. The Bible calls him Satan, while the tempter Lucifer is called Devil. Mephistopholes-Satan attains power over Faust; Lucifer-Devil seduces Eve. These are two magnificent images, of crucial importance for our whole age. They express further that earlier epochs are more marked by Lucifer's imprint, while ours is more under the influence of Satan—the spirit who darkens the earth.

Mankind is also subject to the twofold principle of hardening and dissolution in relation to his place on earth. The West, where hardening is stronger, inclines to deviate towards mechanization whereas the East is predisposed to transports and dreaming. We can see Western man's formative impulse expressed in the nature and cultivation of his individualism. Western civilization is clear, logical, lucid; but it requires spiritual substance if it is not to become only form without content, stiffening in materialism. The shadow of a cosmic hardening force has fallen over the West. The Eastern tendency on the other hand is to an untamed, unbridled soul life. The people are not such strong individualists as in the West but are closer to the general type. The pull here is into formlessness. This is the less differentiated world of Asia with its dark secrets of spirit and blood, with its dreaming, floating kind of soul-being and the charm of magic and occultisms which make it harder for the individual to come to a full awakening of personal consciousness. Lucifer's temptations threaten to enshroud the East.

Between the West, mainly represented by America and its appendages, and the Asiatic East, stands Europe which in this context assumes a special role. Not that Europe is uninfluenced by the two extremes: its special character is rather that it is equally open to both powers and under the constant temptation to swing back and forth between them. This imposes an increased danger, but also a special task.

It may be the human task of Europe to form the spiritual centre, balancing and complementing the opposites and helping to wrest from both poles their positive content.

We can well vizualize this pendulum swing between dissolving and hardening in the cultural polarity of East and West. The adversaries have, each in his own style, made for themselves a kind of beach-head through a process of infiltration. A detailed survey is hardly possible, but through the centuries, the spiritual, social and economic conditions of life in East and West have become impregnated with the specific impulses of the two tempters, affecting in turn the individual. The resulting cultural polarities must not be taken too schematically but understanding the instinctive bias of each—dreaming spirituality on the one hand, materialism on the other—is an important key to their present differences and tensions.

In recent times the primary phenomenon of East-West polarity has been undergoing a remarkable change in that the materialistic impulses no longer remain restricted to the western half of the world but are gaining influence in the East also, as is shown by the continuing inroads of technology into the eastern cultures. This is connected with the fact that during the course of evolution humanity is at one time more susceptible to the Luciferic, and at another to the opposite, tendency.

Thus a further structural order appears. Seen spatially, geographically, evil faces us from East and West. In relation to time, in contrast to the Luciferic inclination of the Middle Ages, the accent is now on the materialistic side. For human nature in general, the two-faced evil is actively experienced in the individual as never before.

The elucidation of the double nature of evil in clear concepts is one of the great deeds of understanding which we owe to Rudolf Steiner. He called the adversaries Lucifer and Ahriman. The fruitfulness of his conceptual differentiation was proved in many spheres of human life. Besides writing and lecturing, he presented the two kinds of evil in artistic form and thereby brought them still nearer in experience. In his *Mystery Plays*, Lucifer and Ahriman appear as spiritual beings speaking and acting as two individuals. One perceives the progress in comparison with Goethe's *Faust*, where both principles are inconclusively combined in Mephistopheles. Rudolf Steiner also created a wooden sculpture, the main figure of which he sometimes called the Representative of Humanity. It depicts Christ at the moment of temptation. With incomparable dignity and purity the Christ figure stands between Lucifer and Ahriman disarming and overcoming them with his gesture of blessing. Through this one can experience the supreme divine archetype of man, who has to reach his humanity through a struggle for equilibrium between the two extremes of error.

The truth of the double nature of evil was well known in earlier times. Temporarily, however, it became lost and it must be recovered again in our time as fundamental for the understanding of evil. The secret was known in the mystery schools of antiquity and was conveyed to the people outside in a cloak of picturesque mythology. From this old mythology certain images and sayings float over to us like

The Two Faces of Evil

a last echo of ancient half-forgotten truths: the Greek image for example of Scylla and Charybdis who dominate either side of a strait and threaten to devour the seafarer. As a last echo of Greek mystery wisdom we find Aristotle's thought that virtue can only be found in wise temperance between two extremes. Perhaps the strange duality of sphinx and pyramid in Egypt also belongs here: the sphinx warning against Lucifer's pull of the mysterious, boundless mystical world; the pyramid an image of the secrets of death and mummification in rigid laws of form. In Germanic mythology the two sides of evil can be found in Loki and the Midgard serpent on the one hand and the Fenris wolf and Hel on the other.

While the New Testament does not explicitly expound the polar relationship between the two forces and the good, it does make clear in differentiating between *Diabolos* and *Satanas* that evil has to be seen as a duality. This has not been considered in the usual theological opinions of the past, owing to the preconceived notion that there is only one kind of evil. The use of a whole series of names for evil, such as Beelzebub, tempter, dragon, snake, beast, Babylon and others, seems to suggest simply cultural or linguistic variation. However with most of these rarer expressions found chiefly in the Book of Revelation, very specific manifestations of evil are indicated.* The New Testament keeps mainly to the use of three words: *Daimonion, Diabolos, Satanas*; these are mentioned more than one hundred times, each word with about the same frequency. Expressions connected with the word *Daimonion* mostly come in descriptions of possessed people and are obviously used where evil in general is meant: whereas passages dealing with *Diabolos* and *Satanas* are very characteristic of the differences we have described. In a few parallel passages the Gospels

* Emil Bock, *The Apocalypse of St. John*, Christian Community Press, London, 19

51

diverge. Matthew and Luke in the temptation scene use the word *Diabolos* while Mark speaks of *Satanas*. Rudolf Steiner described the temptation as a double assault by Lucifer and Ahriman. He explains the desire to accept all the kingdoms of this world as Luciferic; the suggestion to turn stones into bread as Ahriman's attack; and the challenge to leap from the pinnacle of the temple as a combined attack of both powers.* That Mark speaks of *Satanas*, the others of *Diabolos* may serve to confirm this interpretation. In general, Mark seems to have directed his attention more to the Ahrimanic danger and he does not use the word *Diabolos*. Even in the story of the sower, he names *Satanas* while Matthew and Luke again use *Diabolos*. Very revealing in regard to the so-called 'contradictions', and also in general, is the use of two names in the description of the Judas tragedy. John calls the one who incited Judas to his treachery '*Diabolos*', while '*Satanas*' entered into him during the Last Supper. Lucifer is the seducer, Ahriman the executor (John 13:2, 27). Apart from the characteristic way each operates, a general law is here made evident; the influence of the one tempter brings about the fateful appearance of the other. A number of other passages in the Gospels indicate by their presentation, even without special reference to one or the other power, the dual principle of evil.

When Christ is healing the sick the Gospel of Mark relates two deeds taking place in the synagogue at Capernaum. The first healing of all is that of the possessed man (Mark 1:21–28). An 'unclean spirit' which convulses him and cries out is rebuked by Christ and has to leave him. The other report is of the sick man with the withered hand (Mark 3:1–6). It is not hard to recognize the effects of an illness induced by Lucifer in the story about the possessed man. The other man is described as clearly with the symp-

* Rudolf Steiner, *The Fifth Gospel*, Rudolf Steiner Press, London, 1968.

toms of Ahrimanic illness. The facts that follow show that not only those immediately concerned have succumbed to the two kinds of temptation but that many others are exposed to the same danger. After the first healing, rumours are circulated about Christ; an unwholesome excitement affects the crowds and they seem to take his appearance as a sensational happening. The Luciferic, healed in the case of that one man, continues to sound in the many. The Gospel says that after the healing of the man with the shrivelled hand, the Pharisees deliberated how they could kill Christ. Thoughts of murder lurked in their souls; this shows them still unhealed of the Ahrimanic darkening which filled them.

It is strange and certainly not by chance that in the story of the Apostles, both Peter and Paul heal a lame man and overpower a sorcerer. Peter first heals the lame man at the gate of the temple (Acts 3:1–10) and then resists the temptation of the sorcerer Simon (Acts 8:18–25). Paul is first victorious over a sorcerer (Acts 13:8–12) and then over a lame man (Acts 14:8–11). The way in which these stories are told (no other healings by the Apostles are described in such detail) and the double emphasis, call attention to a fundamental law of human evolution: the Apostles, like Christ, have to be led through temptation. They are to heal the Ahrimanic forces which drag down to earth, and in the case of the sick man resulted in his being lame; and they are to integrate into the earthly the tendencies of the 'sorcerer', the Luciferic dreamer, which in an illegitimate manner estrange men from the earth.

The New Testament speaks most powerfully however in wordless language; in the picture of evil at the height of the drama on Golgotha. Christ elevated in the centre between the two thieves. The Gospel does not provide clues to the characters of these two as specifically Luciferic or Ahrimanic: yet the pictorial content itself, the fact that there are two men *between* whom stands the One who overcomes, may perhaps justify the relating of this scene to our problem. In this holiest hour of man's history, nothing occurred that was arbitrary or unimportant. Many criminals have been put to death before and since. The offenders to left and to right of Christ hint at the possibility of amendment at the last and the inexpressible grace of God's Son as he is sacrificing himself. This picture of Christ being nailed to the Cross between the two, which so·infinitely touches the heart in its overpowering grandeur, places the true divine good between the two representatives of evil.

Not through words or concepts but through a picture: behold, O man, God raised between the two who have succumbed to temptation. Thus to raise oneself to the good is to stand between the forces showing the two dangers on the path. Overcome craving for the earth, overcome flight from the earth, and with a gaze directed to Christ awaken the strength for victory over death and devil.

The strength that overcomes evil is Christ's strength, holding the balance between and above the polarity, and transforming temptation for the kingdom of the good.

The many Aspects
of the Fall

We are all accustomed to consider the problem of evil simply as a matter of moral behaviour. Nobody would think of measuring understanding by moral standards, nor do we apply moral yardsticks in artistic matters, because in this case it is not a question of good and evil, but of beautiful and ugly. In education, economy, technology, social life—to mention just a few examples arbitrarily selected—one simply looks at the principles and laws obtaining within the specializations. Morality is not considered. Undoubtedly this distinction is at first justified and necessary to avoid conceptual confusion. On the other hand one cannot penetrate the concept of evil by treating it only as a personal moral situation, isolated from other areas of life. By virtue of its essential nature it is connected with man as a *whole* and not restricted to the moral life alone. It is even part of the camouflage of evil that it appears as if the functions concerned are only of limited importance. It would be a big step forward for men to perceive that in reality world forces are active, striving to grasp the total being of man and that they can more quickly reach their aim the less their intentions are recognized.

Nothing has obscured the nature of evil more than the opinion that it is only one of many phenomena, existing in a corner of human soul life. Evil is not just a private matter for each individual but a spiritual fact of all-embracing importance. Spirituality which is not only restricted to the

55

human brain is always world spirituality and as such permeates all spheres of existence. The Fall has to be recognized as bringing consequences at all levels of human existence and moreover—as the Bible shows—affecting the earth. It is an unspiritual misunderstanding to reduce the Fall to a matter of soul morality: a kind of subjective temptation the individual may easily suffer; but this narrow way of conceiving an event of cosmic dimensions is itself sin. Only a thinking contaminated by the Fall and no longer able to read the magnificent pictures of Genesis could take them literally and materially and reduce them to emotional and religious egotism. We have to regain the lost humility and innocence in order to see the grandeur of the seemingly childish pictures of paradise. A world force outside man, the 'serpent', interfered with human evolution and thereby changed all existence. The 'fields' were cursed; birth and death were placed under new laws and all the conditions of life given a different basis. Lucifer, the fallen but powerful angel, changes the world. Thus the Fall is really a concern of the gods into which man was drawn, as Germanic mythology describes. It was not within human power to resist this temptation and therefore it was not merely a moral failure. The Fall was not a Fall *because* of human sin, but a Fall *into* sin. Lucifer, a cosmic spirit, had to be at work in human nature before men began to commit personal offences. Original sin rests with Lucifer, individual sin with man. If Lucifer had not existed, there would be no personal faults. It was through him that the *possibility* of aberration from the divine good came into the world. But thereby the gift of freedom was created. And because the Fall took place in a higher than human dimension, it could be overcome only by a comparable super-human deed. Each man is responsible for his individual, personal transgressions and has to struggle to overcome them by his own moral efforts; but the predisposition and potential for error extending over and above human measure—that is the 'original sin', which Christ took upon himself and which he overcame. Through the predisposition to sin, individual sin has become possible in the world—through Christ's Deed the original Fall has been redeemed and the possibility created of transforming individual error. The Fall and Golgotha confront each other in a higher realm than man's, in which, however, man has his share. They are both interventions of cosmic importance because they permeate all existence.

With this conception the moral sphere acquires special significance. It is clear that the good is constantly being put in jeopardy by a dark world of shadows: and that dark world is by no means content to be active only in the moral arena, although it makes the most important of its onslaughts there. The adversary is a spiritual principle, able to penetrate man in his entirety, much as a liquid may penetrate through all the pores of a body. The one-sided opinion that only moral dangers are involved actually obstructs insight. Spirit may take on all forms and contents, it is not restricted merely to a few manifestations in the material sphere. In human nature we find it in thoughts and feelings, in moral strivings and artistic conceptions, in the force of memory, in conscience and in many other forms. The seductive force that filters into the human soul may not influence only our actions but can shadow all other functions of soul and spirit. There is therefore justification for speaking of a multiple Fall affecting all levels of human activity.

It may seem strange to look at the capacity for understanding from this point of view, yet here too one must speak of the influence of forces which are against God. Later we shall discuss this matter in more detail. Here it is enough to point out that error can often lead to guilt—think only of what may ensue from the error of a surgeon, a bridge builder or a railway signalman. Errors in recognition can quite obviously attract destructive forces. Evil mysteriously enters if the patient dies, the bridge collapses or the trains collide.

All the parts and functions of human nature are subject to the original disturbance by Lucifer.

The Fall of will means moral decline in the more limited sense of the word 'sin'.

The Fall of thinking means error and lying.

The Fall of feeling means lack of love, cynicism.

The Fall of perception means dullness and over-concern with the material.

The Fall in the realm of life processes means illness.

The Fall in the sphere of the physical body means death.

As a final consequence for the human personality the Fall means obsession.

It is completely inadequate to look for evil only in areas of soul and of morality when the cancer of the Fall induces change in the totality of man's being. Certainly it should not be taken lightly that he can 'sin' in the usual sense, but perhaps the fact of his susceptibility to evil in other fields of his existence is much graver, especially as it generally goes unnoticed. Many of the tragedies of our time do not arise from moral failures but from a vulnerability in other areas which *then* leads to a warping of the moral sense.

Thus not from religious zeal but from sober insight into the being of man, one must speak of an all-penetrating effect of evil. The concept of morality must be widened and its importance be recognized where it has not been understood to apply. A first necessity for our age is to realize the fall of understanding, and a first step in spiritualizing the understanding is to see without prejudice how the separate levels of man's being are penetrated by the forces opposed to God.

Mythologies had this knowledge in a pre-conceptual way; today it has to be rediscovered consciously. Germanic tales for example speak of the three descendants of Loki: the Midgard Snake, the Fenris Wolf, and Hel. In view of the above it is not difficult to understand their meaning. Loki's influence in the human soul shows results in egotism (the Midgard Snake) which brings error and lies (the Fenris Wolf): and within the physical body leads to illness and death (Hel—hell).

The Fall
of the Intellect

The pursuit of knowledge in general and of academic knowledge in particular is concerned with the truth or falsity of its findings but prefers to remain morally neutral in regard to practice or outcome. Where exception is taken to methods or fear of results expressed on moral grounds, this is an inadmissible encroachment on the scientific field. An objective research, as far as possible cleared of intrusion from human considerations, is an ideal of many and has become a criterion of true scientific research. This does away with any responsibility to question related aspects of good or evil. What would be the sense of applying moral criteria to thermodynamics for instance . . . though standards of utility would have relevance. If we look at the repercussions of scientific thinking on human life and human nature, the situation is very different. To take an example from the recent past: the study of genetics has led to important consequences in population control. And however one may view them, the fact remains—and must be emphasized—that they can only be considered appropriate from an isolated scientific aspect.

In Germany, National Socialist rulers brutally exterminated millions of 'worthless' lives. This happened under the influence of what were said to be scientific opinions. But with regard to this branch of science it is perfectly clear that the results cannot be applied without conflict on moral grounds. The difficulty is similar with vivisection:

The Fall of the Intellect

if scientific research is using restraint in this practice it is not because of objections drawn from its own field, but from another outside its domain. Or let us cast a glance at side effects coming from a field of study having no connection with the moral: modern astronomy. In the course of its development astronomy was bound to produce results which let the earth appear in its cosmic insignificance. Some popular writers almost sensuously enjoy the spatial unimportance of our planet. Already Friedrich Schiller was impelled to take a stand against this one-sided conception of the universe: 'Don't gabble on so much about nebulae and suns. Is nature only grand because it lets you count it? Your subject is certainly the grandest in space. But friends, grandeur does not subsist in space.'

The over-emphasis on space that inevitably belittles our earth comes from a hidden materialistic helplessness whose main measure of value and importance is size. As a matter of course this measure is applied to man and pounds into him drastic illustrations of the meaninglessness of his petty existence on our grain of dust. The human being, especially the young person, is imbued with such ideas as early as his schooldays and even though mostly on a subconscious level he suffers a laming of his moral will forces. Higher ideals and religious aims freeze to death under such thoughts. If then are added such conceptions as an insistence on radical genetic and racial theories and the emotions are also engaged, an almost inevitable next step is what we have experienced as the terrible extermination of human life in the concentration camps. In the background, as an unspoken motive or excuse, is the view that this minute speck of our ridiculous little planet is not so important when seen in relation to the universe—and we have stepped from the apparently neutral learning of astronomy to the mass murders of the Third Reich. Needless to add, this is not to hold astronomers responsible: but a fact should be stressed

61

which is not yet clearly enough seen: human nature is a *unity*. A man is not a bundle of juxtaposed isolated systems, that function without reference to each other, but a being whose single parts correspond closely with the wholeness of his personality. If one part suffers so do all the others.

The two-edged nature of research unconcerned with the unity of human nature, becomes frighteningly clear in the aspects opened up by the modern physics which led to the development of the atom bomb. It is said that the research which made the discoveries has nothing to do with their possible misuse; they do not have to be applied in a detrimental way. This hope was entertained for other technical achievements which were later placed in the service of destruction. The question arises whether certain products of the human mind that seem morally neutral do not have a hidden tendency belonging to the moral sphere. Following the history of inventions, one finds that in due course many of them are involuntarily transferred to the service of evil. Is there then justification for speaking of the intellect as neutral in relation to morality? Can it not be that its knowledge inevitably evokes corresponding forces, linked to it in a hidden way and leading automatically to negative consequences? If so, knowledge which only asks 'true or false?' will have a hidden relationship with good and evil.

An older, instinctive wisdom spoke of the seducer who is father both to error and to lies. But while one cannot simply infer from morally evil results that the causative knowledge was in error, it is clear there is a connection between knowledge and morality arising from the unity of human nature itself.

To know the objective side of this relationship, we have to touch on a view which may vex many of our contemporaries.

Man's own ability to understand was initiated by an act of the Luciferic forces. As Prometheus, according to Greek

The Fall of the Intellect

mythology, stole fire from heaven, Lucifer the 'light-bearer' carried the intellectual content of knowledge from divine realms down to earth and made it accessible to man. It is to Lucifer we owe the gift of the light of understanding —and in consequence the impulse for freedom. But because we accepted it from his hands it is a dangerous gift, like a two-edged sword, and continues under the shadow of demonic temptation. The Bible indicates this by presenting the serpent as the seducer who whispers to Adam and Eve to eat the fruit of the tree of knowledge. The mythologies continue the theme and show that the curse of the Fall affected the intelligence: to wit, the Old Testament story of Jacob and Esau. Jacob possesses the gift of cleverness which Esau, who is 'coarser' and closer to nature, does not yet have. Through his intelligence Jacob finds a way to obtain the rights of the firstborn although he was born second. He thereby commits a fraud, but in spite of this he is destined to become the ancestor of the chosen people. The Old Testament obviously acknowledges the gift of intelligence even though it does harbour the danger of moral deviation. A risk has to be taken in view of the goal, which is freedom. At a further stage of development this danger will be overcome. The development of intellect takes place within the tragic process of man's separation *from the divine* which approached its dramatic climax at the beginning of the scientific age. The spiritual aspect of thinking has moved further away from its origin and become increasingly restricted in one-sided application to the spatial and material. In the process, thinking itself has become shrouded in darkness and runs the risk of being seized by the other force of temptation, the Ahrimanic. Human progress demands that intelligence, once estranged from the divine forces, should be reconciled with the spiritual by virtue of man's free deed: otherwise it is taken by Ahriman. Ahriman would like it for himself, to force his spell upon mankind. The battle now being waged is for the renewed *spiritualization of intelligence*. This is one of the keys for understanding our time. If Ahriman were to isolate intelligence and completely sever it from its connection with the divine spiritual world, man would lose his connection with his own spiritual origin and deteriorate into a certainly very clever but purely earthly creature. Those beings who in the interest of the good evolutionary forces are close to man, and as companions of the Archangel Michael are called in Christian terminology Michaelic, are helping to free human thinking from the bonds of the terrestrial and reunite him with the spiritual stream of a higher life. Thus behind the veil of the visible world, a spiritual struggle is taking place and its battlefield is in *human consciousness*. Tradition depicts this conflict as the Archangel Michael's struggle with the Dragon. Man is not placed only passively in this spiritual fight, but actively. Through the nature and content of his thinking he makes himself an organ of spiritual powers, and in striving to permeate his concepts with the living spirit he can become a channel for good divine forces. He becomes a tool of demonic forces if he fills his thinking *only* with the content of the world perceptible to our senses.

More important however than the mere content of thought is the kind of cognition, the 'how' of the thought processes. Abstract, theoretical head thinking, without warmth and without reference to the rest of human nature is at once largely under the domination of Ahriman. This formal thinking, reflecting only impressions of the sense world and spinning a network of one-sided hypotheses around them, is moving further and further away from the total reality of this world. It is great in its grasp of the mineral world, but it fails when applied to what is living and it is incapable of understanding human nature itself. We have made great advances in physics, chemistry and technology, but we are lost in blind alleys in concerns of the

human soul and spirit. Knowledge also succumbs to Ahrimanic influence when it is one-sided and considers its very
one-sidedness as absolute. In this respect even partial
truths become dangerous. They can in fact be even more
dangerous than actual untruths and errors because they are
claimed as true and are in themselves correct. But in so far
as they suppress important parts of the truth they are untrue. The exclusiveness with which quantitative considerations are applied in various disciplines offers a current
example. The purely quantitative-mathematical method is
certainly a very important tool in our effort to understand
the world, but it is only one among many others which
must also be used if we are not to move completely away
from the qualitative nature of the whole world. A one-
sided mathematical way of thinking is penetrating all
science and through a tyrannical claim to exclusiveness it
paralyses progress in understanding the spiritual and the
qualitative. Even in physics where the mathematical method
can celebrate such triumphs, progress has been paid for by
loss of an understanding of the qualitative. W. Heisenberg
writes: 'I have tried to explain how physics and chemistry—
propelled by we don't know what power—have constantly
developed further in the direction of a mathematical analysis
of nature with the aim of cohesiveness. Our sciences'
desire for an understanding of nature in the original sense of
the word has thereby become less and less'.*

Heisenberg says 'propelled by we don't know what
power'. We must answer: that power which forces man to
cultivate a formalist view of the world at the expense of
knowledge of the qualities involved; the Ahrimanic force,
which severs him from the complete reality. It could be
childish to fear the mathematical method as such and
deride it as demonic. However, its claim to be the only

* *Philosophic Problems of Nuclear Science*, translated by F. G. Hayes, London,
1952.

valid method and its disregard of that mode of understanding fostered by Goethe and developed further by
Rudolf Steiner has had severe and tragic consequences. It
is an invitation to Ahriman. By artificially eliminating all
qualitative considerations and arbitrarily abstracting one
aspect of the whole, a spiritual vacuum is created into
which the Ahrimanic can enter.

Now we have come closer to illumining the problem,
still left open, of the inner connection between certain kinds
of thinking and their moral consequences. The above
examples, to which we could easily add, show that certain
concepts and ways of thinking have effects on human
behaviour leading almost inevitably to moral deviations.
Consideration of the cosmos purely in mathematical terms
is destructive for the ideals of humanity; perception of only
the physical and disregard of the spiritual being of man carries
the seeds of inhumanity. This is the deeper basis of many
phenomena of the present time where seemingly innocent
thoughts cause catastrophic results within the moral sphere.
Ahriman, entering the inner self of man, produces results
that nobody wanted or intended. The bestiality, sadism
and inhumanity of the last decades, the anonymity of its
perpetration, is due to the development of consciousness in
recent centuries.

Our analysis should not be understood as a criticism of the
modern drive for scientific discovery. The development of
modern consciousness corresponds to a deep inner necessity
with which we are in wholehearted sympathy. From it has
flowed what is great and valuable in our times. The exact-
ness, clarity and purity of selfless scientific research are of
the utmost importance to the maturing of human nature.
That Ahrimanic forces have infiltrated human understanding is a tragic mystery, and yet an inevitable step that
must be positively encountered. Only vague dreamers or
blind leaders of the blind who would keep men in medieval

innocence could wish away intellectual advance. Intellect becomes dangerous only when held to be absolute and the only salvation. When we have harvested its fruits, we must grow above and beyond it.

With the introduction of automation into the combination, digestion and storing of intellectual-conceptual information, the discussion of intelligence enters a new stage. Technicians concerned with computers like to use a terminology previously reserved for human activity. They talk about their machines not only recognizing signs and making logical combinations but also having an ability to memorize and learn. People ascribe intelligence to these machines; conversely an endeavour is made to explain human soul life in terms of the computer.

It is revealing to see how the English mathematician A. M. Turing thinks with regard to this subject. He suggests an 'imitation game' in which the examiner confronts an invisible partner with whom he is only indirectly in contact. He has to give his unknown opponent tasks—mathematical, logical, comparing, evaluating etc.—within a frame of reference established before the game. If on the basis of the answers given he is unable to decide whether the reply is given by a human being or a machine then, says Turing, it would be permissible to ascribe 'intelligence' to the automaton taking part in the game.

This example takes us into the controversy surrounding the effort to deduce the characteristics of the human mind from physically known facts. One of the most energetic representatives of these attempts is Professor Steinbuch who rejects the assumption that 'to explain mental functions, presuppositions must be made which go beyond normal physics'.*

A major argument against acceptance of 'artificial intelligence' is that the abilities of an electronic brain have first

* Karl Steinbuch, *Automat und Mensch*, Springer Verlag, Berlin, 1961.

67

to be given to it by its creator; because each apparatus has to be not only constructed but programmed by a human being, it is not possible to get more out of it than has been programmed into it. Karl Steinbuch answers: 'The difference between programming an automaton for highly sophisticated activity and the training of an apprentice for any kind of profession seems to me very slight'. Moreover, man as a 'learning system' can be understood without the aid of facts beyond the physical, simply by assuming chance organization and natural selection. One of the basic motives which developed over billions of years, he says, would be the survival of the species which, as a prime standing order, determines human behaviour. Adjuncts can be deduced from this central motive of preservation: the will to learn, etc. Systematic learning consists in improving the internal model of the external world by experience. Intelligence, he concludes, is a human invention, anticipating the results of natural selection without exposing the individuals to danger or even sacrificing them.

In attempting to relate human intelligence as closely as possible to the functioning of data processing machines and to explain one by the other, Steinbuch says: 'What we can observe as mental functions in man is the receiving, digesting, storing and imparting of information'. He is well aware that this by no means explains all soul functions. Therefore he introduces a concept of the 'economic principle' to cover a number of additional activities of human life. Since for him all processes of the soul are closely bound to the switchboard brain, he supposes that in the effort to switch and change signals the brain system has become adjusted by natural selection to operate the flow of information with minimal effort. To this end condensations are prepared, or sub-programmes are included for simplification. 'Feeling' is the combined experience of a group of functions of our body and of our thinking apparatus.

The Fall of the Intellect

Nature proceeds economically when changing the levers: 'I would like to declare the two concepts "like" and "dislike" as standing orders stored as follows: *like*: repeat the actions which led to this result, your behaviour does not need to be changed, relax; *dislike*: avoid the action which has led to this result, you have to change your behaviour and make effort'. Faithfulness would sometimes be 'the result of lack of ability to change rather than of ethical influences'. Happiness 'seems to be a complex of information saying that the internal model has been satisfactory and therefore no change of signals is necessary'. The drive for power can be understood as avoidance of the need to change signals. The internal model is not readjusted to the environment, but the environment to the model. The concept of 'harmony' also, which plays such a large role in aesthetic statements, could probably, according to Steinbuch, be traced back to the economical utilization of human reflexes.

We have quoted a number of statements showing how a man steeped in modern technology approaches the problem of intelligence. It is quite apparent that here the theories of Buechner, Moleschott, Haeckel and others, presented with innocent naïvety about a hundred years ago, have through the reality of technical facts acquired a dynamic which makes them as convincing as the atomic bomb of atomic theory. Even if some of the sentences quoted sound grotesque today, it must be realized that technology and the manipulation of man that accompanies it will ensure that such views gain increasing confirmation through being applied. A case in point is Steinbuch's statement that 'the well-known fact that states of emotion can be effectively changed by drugs seems to be a strong argument for the physical reality of emotions'.

May intelligence be ascribed to machines, and how far can the functions of the human mind be explained as physical processes? Today cybernetics is almost able to construct machines which can have independent 'experience'. These machines are given the model of a small sector of the environment: they try out different theoretical responses to environmental stimuli in order to select the most suitable, which will then be carried out. Or they differentiate between important and unimportant experiences and erase the unimportant from their 'memory'; in this way they can control and if necessary correct themselves. Machines are being developed to 'read' signs—letters, numbers etc., written mechanically or even by hand—and then digest the content of the writing. Others are designed to produce translations of different languages, etc. One may feel that the controversy over the intelligence of machines versus human intelligence is idle play with words: 'The mousetrap has a certain intelligence since it does not snap shut for a fly, a bee or a bumble-bee but awaits a sufficiently heavy object such as a mouse.' The important point is to recognize that with cybernetics intelligence is implanted in the machine. Although to a certain extent this applies to every machine, it does so only fully to computers, which are, as it were, direct copies of human intelligence and its way of functioning. There is no sense whatever in denying the evident similarity between intellectual thinking and machine 'thinking'. The electronic machine is a replica of a certain human ability and it can be utilized to understand this ability but it must be realized that this very specific and one-sided action represents only a limited area of mental possibility. Moreover, it should be taken into account that this faculty of intellectual thinking is a child of our own time and is already on the decline. Intelligence was once at a height which can no longer be reached. The modern intellect is only the lifeless shadow of a force that connected men with their spiritual origins. Once there was a thinking that was experienced as the divine breath—pneuma. The remnants of it can still be sensed, for example

The Fall of the Intellect

in Plato's works. This 'thinking' was *inspired*, that is to say, *breathed into* man. Its occurrence, its laws and the whole way in which it appeared was independent of any switchboard brain. Hence there could be no way of comparing it to the functioning of electrical machines. Conversely it could not have invented or constructed such machines. That has been reserved for our time, when the human soul has been fastened to the human body much as Prometheus was chained to the rock; and the thinking can only take place through the switchboard of the nervous system and, tied to this, it cannot see the spiritual in any other way than in pictures which resemble the material! One must therefore say the scientists are right who view the brain as a complicated switchboard of electrical technology. As far as purely intellectual thinking is concerned there is no difference in principle between connections involving resistors, condensers, transistors etc. and the function of the roughly fifteen billion neurons of the nervous system (although we do not yet know in all detail how this mechanism works). The fact must be recognized today, but man has no reason to brag about this insight. His need of the brain as an instrument of his spirit, and the (more or less measurable) intellectual processes of the nervous system bind the human spirit to matter. *This is the direct result of the Fall.*

We cannot share the triumphant attitude of scientists who are delighted to have explained the process of human thinking in terms of an electronic brain. With their explanation they have unwittingly made a religious discovery. For a man rightly understanding his own development would have to hide his head in shame and tell himself: men have fallen so far into this state of lifeless matter that they must now explain their noblest faculty in terms of mechanisms. Any talk of ideals as in the past is inapplicable to a condition of such objective human poverty—the scientists are tragically right!

In this situation the question can only be: how can human thinking be freed from its bondage to matter? Certainly not by becoming intoxicated with the relative correctness of the theory described. Certainly not by turning disdainfully away from science and deriding its devotees as 'materialists'. The important step would be to experience the religious core of this tragedy of our time and to glean strength for a new departure from painful familiarity with such a truth. As it was possible for the human soul to fall, so there is hope that it may rise again.

We hear much talk today about the decline in morality and it is commonly believed that moral strength can be increased by appeals to good will. In fact it can be influenced only by our whole life of thought and feeling. In earlier times the strengthening forces came as a matter of course from the pertaining world view, which drew sustenance from its religious link with the divine world so long as a unity of thinking and belief still existed. This unity has been destroyed with the decline of the older world view. Thinking went its own way and religious belief sought to preserve its own domain apart from thinking. If it is not possible to reunite understanding honestly with belief and thereby bridge the split in human nature, it will not be possible to rejuvenate the element which builds morality. Religious belief, fearfully rejecting understanding, can no longer build up morality, and as we have described, Ahrimanic effects flowing from a thinking severed from the unity of the world are incessantly destroying it. For a time the separation of knowledge and belief could exist without causing moral decline; but now we see with terrible clarity how with steady acceleration moral inhibitions are swept away as forces of consciousness prove stronger than religious feeling. The human being, designed as a unity, can no longer bear the inner contradiction and his moral will retreats before the demonic onslaught. Only a fundamental change

The Fall of the Intellect

of consciousness, involving both the *content* and the *structure* of our intellectual powers, will be able to stem the oncoming danger. This change lies in a way of thinking which must transcend the formal, statistical and quantitative delimitations, reaching an all-embracing, all-human method that includes the qualitative. Goethe strove for such a method. Rudolf Steiner established it and developed it further. Such thinking is capable of uniting with the nature of the divine good, whose power it can reveal. Filled with truly spiritual content it can stimulate the forces necessary for overcoming our present crisis. Needless to say, this is not a question of a single deed since to a greater or lesser degree intellectualism is a deeply ingrained habit in us all. Good intentions do not suffice, only continuous efforts at self-education over many years. As a cultural factor this new mode of consciousness will not appear until education through school and university is no longer a mere accumulation of knowledge, but brings thinking, feeling and willing to harmonious development.

Insight into how the Ahrimanic forces of evil infiltrate human nature through the one-sidedness of knowledge is only *one* step towards a deeper understanding of the mystery of evil. We have to supplement this insight from other angles to come closer to the core of the problem.

There are many channels for the Ahrimanic to stream into man. As a supersensible element it cannot achieve a direct foothold in the earthly but for its purpose uses man, who through his spiritual content is connected with the supersensible and, on the other hand, through his incorporation in a physical body has a share in the earth. How far Ahriman will be able to appear on earth will depend to a large degree on how men use their freedom. Thus the phenomenon of evil is a subjective concern, but at the same time an objective fact. Its manifestation is humanly-subjective in nature: its content is a cosmic factor reaching far beyond the individual.

The Nature of Evil

To approach more nearly the question of the nature of evil and its importance in the world we must form a concept foreign to the thought habits and prejudices of our time: that of purely spiritual supersensible being. In earlier times a visionary consciousness must have been very common and very widespread. How else can we explain the natural, uninhibited way in which people spoke of spirits of different kinds, angels and demons and elemental beings? It is convenient to shrug off the wealth of such references as 'imaginative folk fantasies', for the old mode of visionary cognition has long since been replaced by sense perception and a conceptual consciousness and only a few atavistic and unhealthy remnants of visionary experience still persist. We can no longer relate directly to those ways, nor to a dogmatic presentation of systems of belief, such as that of the orders of angels. To engage in metaphysical speculation on such subjects is equally futile; but a third path open to our time is given in Anthroposophy by Rudolf Steiner. By means of the training in cognition it describes, a heightened consciousness can be reached which allows objective, unemotional perception of non-physical beings and whereby human consciousness changes into the consciousness of these beings. Afterwards such experience can be translated into our familiar language of rational thinking and thus be made accessible to us even though we ourselves do not have it. Denial of such experience proceeds neither from facts nor logic but from certain habits of thinking and from opinions made firm by custom.

The Nature of Evil

The descriptions of spiritual beings given in Anthroposophy bear certain resemblances to those of spiritual hierarchies in early Christian times. This is why Rudolf Steiner frequently used these familiar terms. All the hierarchies of spiritual beings evolve in the course of vast time rhythms, or rounds, during which the beings in their different ways progress to new forms of consciousness and new tasks. An important fact for our subject is that not all spiritual beings have progressed 'normally' in their development but some are cosmically 'retarded'. They did not pass through certain stages in step with others of equal rank but delayed the execution of tasks given to them and so retarded their state of consciousness. To have thus fallen behind in relation to other orders in a time sense also causes an important shift in power. Since all hierarchies are involved in the evolution of the divine world and are closely interwoven the effects reach to everything in existence, including of course man. The beings which have taken an irregular stance in relation to world development have different intentions towards man from those progressing along the 'normal' path. Luciferic and Ahrimanic beings have remained at previous stages of development and now seek to give impulses which would have been justified earlier but are misplaced at a later stage. We may see Lucifer and Ahriman as leading spirits of two groups of 'fallen' angels. The following comparison may be permitted. To give food meant for adults to a baby, or for a grown-up to go on playing the games of his childhood would, as well as being a time shift, be detrimental. As the Luciferic-Ahrimanic beings try to force their impulses on man they become dangerous for him because of their own displacement in the cosmos. In this sense they have to be classified as 'evil'. August Strindberg came surprisingly close to this truth in his brilliant aphorism: 'When gods age they become demons'. At the same time it becomes clear that this process is not absolute. Like all hierarchical beings they have a world task to perform. It is only in certain regards that Lucifer and Ahriman are 'in the wrong place' relative to the earth, and so for man, who is unprepared, become evil entities. He must not passively yield to their power but in the struggle with them must follow the aims given him by the Godhead. It is possible to understand that hierarchies in progressing 'normally' could not have accomplished certain intentions for man if an element of resistance had not been included in the course of his general development. Retardation of certain beings served to create opposing forces for others. Through the ensuing conflicts higher abilities could arise than would otherwise have been possible. The *law of polarity and enhancement* is evident here, assisting completion of the divine plan of the world. Goethe once said death was nature's trick for having more life. So may we say: evil is the trick of the gods for a greater good.

Thus far evil is 'intended by God'. From a higher viewpoint some hierarchical groups can be seen as making a kind of cosmic sacrifice so that the world may progress. Nevertheless man may not yield to the influence of his adversaries but in recognition he must endeavour to wrest good from them. Evil thereby receives a certain justification. The world cannot be imagined without it, yet Lucifer and Ahriman will have done good service to a maturing humanity if men will recognize the cosmic trespass as temptation and become able to reject it. A complicated relationship appears. Apart from these indirect tasks, the powers of evil are pursuing their own development. The simplistic distinction between good and evil may have sufficed in earlier times. Our age calls for more specific concepts since without detailed understanding the difficulties of this life cannot be mastered. To understand the justification, within limits, of the evil powers needs a heightened sense of responsibility, otherwise its dangerous truth could be a temptation to underestimate the seriousness of evil. When we talk of the necessity and even the justification of evil, we attain to a view held by the divine world. Man may hold it only when, with reverence, he takes God's world-thoughts into his thinking and when he raises himself to spiritual insight. He must be aware that with the other part of his being, as earthly man, he does not reach this level.

It may now be clear that the final aim of the confrontation with evil cannot be its destruction, since there are beings and forces concerned which cannot be called evil in absolute terms. In the sense of a divine world economy it may emerge that the highest aim is to re-integrate the direction of effectiveness of the adverse powers into the harmonious stream of cosmic development. With this we touch on a secret which should not be spoken of without a certain awe: the redemption of evil. As far as man is called on to share in this in the future, his contribution will consist of accomplishing within himself, in conscious self-awareness and self-discipline, the transformation and sublimation of these forces. Their future redemption is prepared not by asceticism and deadening, but by transubstantiation of the cosmically shifted and improperly placed forces of evil. Thereby we would return to them what we have received from them indirectly through their sacrifice.

Ahrimanic Influences
and Possession

We have shown that evil appears not only directly through human actions but also through the operations of the machinery of civilization. People are being manipulated, organized and administered, suffering many hardships which nobody consciously intended. These are consequences of political, administrative and bureaucratic institutions in which evil can establish itself impersonally and objectively. We have further seen at how many places on this earth such hopeless situations have arisen and continue to arise. The insoluble problems give the adversaries the opportunity to create more confusion and trouble.

The first step in the Luciferic and Ahrimanic penetration by way of a one-sided approach to knowledge, influences moral foundations. The second is taken when indirectly by way of Ahrimanic thinking, the whole machinery of civilization is permeated with Ahrimanic spirituality. Today we have to bear the results of the 'intellectual Fall' in social, political and economic life, for the materialistic thoughts of the nineteenth century, which then were only theory in people's heads, have now become reality. Consequences are bound to arise if we think man is only a highly developed animal or a complicated machine; we are harvesting the fruit of this kind of thinking in the present treatment of millions of people as if they were animals or machines. Most of our cultural and social institutions have been encompassed or influenced by similar materialistic thoughts. There is no such thing as a 'theoretical' spirit one may adopt trustingly and without consequences, according to the adage that 'thoughts are free' and since 'only' ideas are concerned and not reality. Everything mental-spiritual has practical consequences, deriving as it does from a reality higher than what is visibly existent; the latter is only the result of the former. In the catastrophic consequences of nineteenth-century thinking, the Ahrimanic has created an actual revelation of itself; for everything spiritual is surging towards revelation and endeavours to create a true image of itself in the world. The impersonal anonymity of automation, the de-personalization and de-humanization of conditions of life and the levelling of existence are steps in a kind of embodiment of the Ahrimanic spirit. In his struggle for humanity the man of today must not only be aware of the dangers from within himself, but must also encounter the organs of Ahrimanic activity in the impersonal arrangements of society. When Goethe let Faust become financial adviser, a man of technology and a social reformer on a grand scale under the influence of Mephistopheles, he gave a prophetic picture. Faust conjures up new evil and entangles himself in further guilt in spite of his best intentions.

Beyond these two steps in the Ahrimanic inspiration of our consciousness and culture, the beginnings of a further invasion of it are becoming evident. The danger is that the Ahrimanic not only appears as the shadow-like companion and executive of emancipated intelligence, but independently uses the total body-soul organization of individuals to the exclusion of their own personality. The total estrangement of personality is threatened: a defeat of the unifying forces which normally direct and are responsible for all human functions. With each harmless moral temptation we can notice how a foreign element pushes its way into our ego, urging it to a particular action. In such a case the centre of personality is generally still involved; although subjugated it is not suppressed completely and feels the process as shame or a pang of conscience. The further invasion accelerates the extraneous influence: conscience is dulled, a partial paralysis is threatened or even entire loss of awareness. This process of increasing alienation is already happening in many ways and degrees as statistics confirm. In the experience of pastors, psychotherapists and criminologists, there is an increase of cases where people say they felt prompted to do something that was against their own will but they had to do these particular actions as if sleepwalking and did not become fully aware of them until later. A further cause for concern arises through borderline cases not yet directly counted among psychological illnesses since they do not lead to criminal acts. Their number is appallingly high as one knows from experience as well as from reports and research. They are found in everyday life. It seems that well educated people are especially susceptible, groups who are the custodians of modern intellectualism and thus the most exposed to the Ahrimanic clouding of consciousness. One can perceive this cause behind a large number of 'nervous breakdowns' in a seemingly protected milieu, disturbances of psychological equilibrium, neuroses and, among other outcrops, half-schizophrenic compulsive acts. Mostly the afflicted people can keep these uncontrolled actions within tolerable limits; or they may hide them so that often not even the closest relatives become aware of them. They very rarely speak to others about their predicament, presumably because they are 'embarrassed', or because they do not want to admit it to themselves. Hence the number of these sick men and women may be much higher than is generally known. What in earlier times occurred as a rare exception is now becoming an all too common sympton of decline. Highly esteemed people in socially respected positions and often with considerable gifts, pursue a secret double life often leading them to questionable acts and moral decline. The newspapers are full of reports of such double lives, exposed through some accidental circumstance. The deviations are not necessarily criminal or utterly immoral; irregularities, rather, that do not bring the doer into conflict with the law. Gambling, alcoholism, narcotic addiction and sexuality are the most prevalent forms. These are indeed old and well-known temptations and as such should not be overestimated. It is their widespread extent and their appearance in otherwise well-balanced people which is new. Particularly among the well educated, there are men and women who accept the estrangement of their being as something perfectly normal. They may justify themselves if at all by saying that they need such 'relaxations' from time to time. The comment made by Dr. Fuchs is most revealing. During his trial for atomic espionage he referred to his behaviour in a totally different sphere as a kind of 'controlled schizophrenia'. Apparently he believed that one could as it were simultaneously 'travel on two tracks'—but sooner or later the human being is thereby split.

What is it that underlies this inclination to live with a double? It appears to be so general that next to the concept of 'collective guilt' one is tempted to set that of 'collective susceptibility'. We have called the first two steps of the infiltration of anti-God forces into our time the Ahrimanic inspiration of consciousness and culture. In view of the phenomenon of men acting under the partial exclusion of their own will, as if they are the instrument of tendencies originating outside them, we must speak of the third step as a kind of 'incarnation', an embodiment of Ahrimanic beings.

The process of permeation by the Ahrimanic principle can be compared with an influence transmitted from one human being to another. Much of the influence may be lessened or neutralized through consciousness but on the other hand, in the case of an 'incarnation', soul, spirit and will are directly seized for a certain period of time. The Ahrimanic entity sinks into the total soul and body organization and may eliminate self-consciousness and temporarily take possession of it. This embodiment can be unhesitatingly aligned with the concept of 'possession'. In such states it is not the person himself who thinks, speaks and acts, but a demonic intelligence which seizes him and makes use of his soul and physical part. This might seem a mythological way of looking at the question, but we hope to have shown that without resort to mythology, sober, factual concepts can be developed to explain the existing phenomena. In hypnotic suggestion for example, the ego-consciousness of the subject is switched off during the trance and the clearly recognizable mind and will of the hypnotist is substituted. If the concept of a spiritual being is admitted at all, there should be no difficulty in conceiving the incorporation into a human being. Moreover, the events in Nazi Germany have provided many additional examples to support this explanation. In our opinion there is no other way of understanding the shocking deeds in the concentration camps than through the idea of possession. Demons were there in power and were temporarily able to take mass possession of human souls. Nothing in such a view imposes on our reason. The greatest and most urgent riddle is the fact that those who tortured hundreds and thousands to death were themselves human beings of flesh and blood. They were fathers of families who loved their wives and children as we do. They were sons and daughters who in common with the rest of us loved their mothers—and yet, without compunction, they slaughtered men, women and children who were linked to loved ones in just the same way. Seeing those people later before the judges, one was often astounded by the seemingly quite harmless and average types where one had perhaps expected satanic features.

Ahrimanic Influences and Possession

Something similar applies to Adolf Hitler. He cannot be said to have had a 'demonic' face. On the contrary, especially in his early years, it was the face of an apparently ordinary, unremarkable citizen. What is happening here? Innocent appearance does not contradict our theory but rather confirms it. As here explained, possession is not a startling and wondrous event where the devil appears in hooves and cock's feathers and the air is filled with the stench of pitch and sulphur. It is a well camouflaged process, a temporary incarnation of Ahrimanic forces. A man's personal ways, his good and bad habits, are not eliminated, only for the time being exaggerated to the demonic. Afterwards the afflicted one returns to his previous state and only a weakened condition remains, making him receptive to further, gradually deepening incorporations of the demonic forces.

What are the preconditions of these phenomena? The general conditions have been described. The gradual penetration of a human consciousness prepares the way but other factors bring about the actual possession. The comparison with hypnosis may help us here. The hypnotic elimination of will can take place only if normal consciousness can be dimmed. Something similar must happen to bring about possession by superhuman entities. The alert ego-consciousness has to be put to sleep and be replaced by another for such exceptional conditions to operate. Normally, a wide-awake consciousness can confront alien influences and so resist them without much trouble. It is not until the normal structure of spirit-soul-and-body is disturbed by a reduced ability to perceive and judge critically and rationally that the influences can make themselves felt. Conditions of fainting and lessening of consciousness are the best preconditions for this; not so much those which sometimes accompany physical weakness but rather weakness of the ego, the I. This does not mean the lower, selfish ego, but the true, 'higher ego'. The former may even be strongly developed and yet an ego-weakness be present. In the habits of modern life only the earthly ego-image is considered and the true ego-forces which are nourished only through their living connection with the divine world are weakened. Where their action is disrupted or disturbed, a foreign 'ego' can enter man, whether through hypnosis or other unauthorized suggestion, or as a superhuman entity.

The factor of ego-weakness is an exceedingly serious problem, related to the numerous phenomena of decline in our civilization. The most important causes of weakness of the ego are intellectualism and materialism with their unhealthy consequences in exaggerated technological and mechanical influences. Franz Werfel referred in a lecture* to the 'taking away of the reality' of this world through technology: it eliminates one half of existence, namely the spiritual, which belongs to reality as much as does the material. A complete pathology of civilization would be needed to characterize the innumerable contributory factors undermining wakeful ego-consciousness. Suffice it to point out how thoughtless use of cinema, TV and radio, creates very serious impediment for the will of the individual. A human being subjected for hours daily through decades to the sound of a radio to which he is only half listening drives out his higher capacities. A similar effect is caused by various other excesses of our society if no counterbalance is created by the conscious inner effort of the individual. The ego retreats after the rape of its tender nature and thus, slowly, a spiritual vacuum develops within. Ahrimanic forces may then enter. An immeasurable danger for mankind is being brought about in this way. The process of demonization which has begun is of far greater proportion than the earlier immorality of emotion and desire. The problem of evil is

---

* *Realismus und Innerlichkeit*, Zsolnay-Verlag, 1931.

84

now more than a moral dilemma, because evil itself as an actual entity is being called on to the stage of the human soul. At this point it is appropriate to refer to a historical fact which has considerably contributed to this crisis. During the centuries before and immediately after Christ, an image of man was cultivated which emphasized his inner connection with the divine world. Without question it means much for the entire feeling of existence if a man—even only as philosophic speculation—can feel that part of his being is in true communion with the divine. That was the feeling of cultured people until the eighth and ninth centuries before it was severely shaken by theological dogmatism. The old teaching of the threefold body, soul and spirit was declared to be heresy and was gradually done away with by the Church, with threat of heavy penalties. Through a clever terminology, the entire man was actually declared spiritually incompetent when he was denied the spiritual part of his being. After that, all theologians had to teach according to the dogma that man consists only of body and soul, the soul having spiritual properties; and the consciousness of a spiritual principle dwelling within, already weakened, was finally completely lost.

It is a fact that regardless of the intention, the ground was prepared through the Church for a world-view in which the subsequent materialism of the natural sciences could continue. Man was deprived at a stroke of his spiritual ego and the door was thereby opened for doubts of a direct connection between God and his own spiritual nature. It is naïve to think that the Church guarded man's religion; in reality it undermined the foundation of religion. For consciousness, a vacuum resulted, similar to that which has followed intellectualism in the theoretical sphere and has damaged the practical course of civilization.

Here the circle of theory and practice, of ideas and reality, closes. If the spiritual emptiness is not filled in a way appropriate to man through his own spiritual ego-strengthening, it is used by demons as a gateway for their assault. One can compare this process with certain chemical reactions. If an element of a chemical compound is artificially driven out, another may take its place because the reduced compound tends eagerly to absorb another element to fill the void. Comparably in man, if the spiritual member is forced out of its harmony with soul and body, the inescapable tendency exists to draw in a spirituality from outside. The Ahrimanic entities are just waiting for such opportunities for entry. Then, as a dark double, the foreign spiritual element can work within and make use of a man's other faculties. We experienced the first terrible results of Ahrimanic possession in the demonic deeds of the concentration camps. They were not caused by a normal lapse of morality in weak individuals but must be seen in their context of the general human situation. Nothing is really gained by punishing such people for this is less a matter of morality and law than of ministry and medicine. A fundamental reconsideration by mankind is necessary if such catastrophes are not to occur on a larger scale. Paul's words acquire distressing importance for our time: 'For we are not contending against flesh and blood, but against the principalities, against the powers, against the world rulers of this present darkness, against the spiritual hosts of wickedness in the heavenly places.' (Eph.6:12). Such words may once have sounded like over-enthusiastic religious fantasy; today we realize their sombre truth.

For the one thus afflicted, possession by the Ahrimanic spirit represents an extension and intensification of his entire existence. All his abilities and talents become much greater through his incorporation of a being so far above man. He may not at first appear to be the sick person that in a deeper sense he is. Quite the contrary! He will appear as if rejuvenated and invigorated. He will become more productive and be full of activity, with energy and stamina probably far above the average. He will bubble over with new thoughts and ideas and show all the signs of real genius. His influence over other men can grow thereby astoundingly. Many will be affected by the suggestive power of his speech, and the effects of his work will be difficult to escape. Why shouldn't the masses run after him? He is undoubtedly a genius—it all comes easily to him and he wins people's hearts. But he is a genius by the grace of Ahriman. It would be a mistake however to believe that everything he says and does is false and untrue or base and evil. Many partial truths will be cleverly used to conceal the fact that deep down he is a representative of the lie. Ahriman is a being of the highest intelligence who does not make his appearance as crudely as we may have imagined the devil to do. A subtle ability for disguise matches a great but cold intelligence and where he speaks it will become more and more difficult to distinguish the relative good and right from evil and wrong, the lie from the truth.

How are we to recognize that we contend not just with a person but with a much higher intelligence? There is no simple formula for this. Anyone smugly supposing he could certainly size up such a character might well be among the most easily deceived. Persons subject to possession may possibly be recognized by an unusual instability. Temporary periods of undeniable genius and an astonishing intensity in their whole behaviour will alternate with others when they sink back as if empty and quite burned out. A swinging between dynamic displays of strength and exhausted numbness, uncommon to such a degree with normal people, will be unavoidable for them since it is only from time to time that they are taken over by the one who inspires and incarnates in them. It is possible however that in future such cases of incarnation will be less noticeable and something else will appear as criterion of the condition.

We mentioned above that a continuous exchange takes place between Lucifer and Ahriman; one follows the other. Thus Lucifer too will be evoked by the presence of Ahriman and will find ways to excite emotion and passion to fever pitch in those afflicted. By such combined action people's morality will be undermined. They will fall prey to lies and vanity in exceptional degree, be filled with unbridled passions or live with utter egotism. When asked how one could be sure of distinguishing masters of deception from the spiritual being of Christ, Rudolf Steiner once answered: 'Christ is the purest selflessness'. Such an answer will give the power to distinguish them, even when the Luciferic and Ahrimanic beings appear in Christian camouflage. Men overshadowed by these spirits are liable to succumb to delusions of grandeur like the Caesars or they may become totally insane.

The Coming of Antichrist

If it appears that in the previous chapter we have painted a theoretical, futuristic picture and occasionally coloured it too boldly, we must stress again and again that many of the things said are already history. We have experienced the slaughter and other effects of war whose frightfulness can only be understood as a result of possession in people prepared by Ahrimanic beings. And yet all this can only be considered as prelude to a still stronger demonic attack, the culmination of which will be the appearance of the Antichrist.

The prophecy of the coming of Antichrist has been considered a fable and has spawned many absurdities. Anyone inclining to the sensational and to mystical excitement may become subject to further unhealthy and fantastic excesses. The history of Christendom knows a whole series of epidemic mass psychoses prompted by a supposed arrival of Antichrist. In addition, a tendency arose to see the expected enemy of God in historical personalities by whom Christendom felt threatened. Thus the mysterious reference to the number 666 in the Book of Revelation was interpreted as indicating Nero. More recent times have taken their own short cuts in this matter: the Hussites and Reformers saw the Pope as Antichrist, others recognized him in the rule of the Turks, or in Napoleon, Hitler and others.

In face of such notions, the rationalist of today believes he may put the idea altogether aside as a foolish exaggeration of the over-susceptible. Yet scepticism is no better basis than superstition for an understanding of Christian prophecy. The content of the Antichrist idea falls either toward the Luciferic or the Ahrimanic interpretation. A soul too prone to Luciferic enthusiasms inflates the idea to uncritical fantasy; a mind governed by Ahrimanic scepticism is prey to spiritual blindness in its disbelief.

The prophecy of the appearance of the Antichrist goes back to Christ himself, who gave his disciples this secret like a last testament during the instruction on the Mount of Olives. In particularly sombre words he unveiled for them a part of the future when the great crisis of humanity will occur; when the individual will decide to remain connected with Christ or will follow the adversary. Of the many signs to come in those days Christ indicated three which are of special importance in the hour of Antichrist. The 'desolating sacrilege' will stand in the holy place (Matt. 24:15): men will appear, claiming to be Christ, and false prophets will arise. The desolating sacrilege is an apocalyptic image, which appears in the Book of Daniel to which Christ clearly refers. It is the archetype of the violation of the Holy of Holies. The altar is desecrated and misused. Where in the imagery of ritual the wings of the cherubim reveal the presence of the highest angels, demons will be worshipped. The cult and the sacrament of the altar, the centre of God's presence and activity, will be despoiled to invoke the forces of darkness as sacramental acts are turned into their demonic counterparts with conscious evil intent. The 'desolating sacrilege' is a pictorial way of saying that men will fall prey to black magic on the grandest scale. Modern man hardly knows what is to be understood by this. He may think of the busy secrecy of a charlatan with unsavoury intrigues and perversities; but real black magic, which so far is limited in extent, has for its goal rituals invoking the direct presence of Ahrimanic powers. It seeks to further the incarnation of Ahriman. And this must be kept in mind when thinking of the desolating sacrilege.

The Coming of Antichrist

False prophets are not merely strange, usually fanatical but harmless dreamers who appear in various places and make speeches in order to save the world and win over some naïve minds. It is said of them that they will perform signs and miracles. We have to see them as people of the highest Ahrimanic intelligence and Luciferic genius. In their way they will have the gift of supersensible insight and have strong supersensible powers at their disposal. They will not be active only in the religious sphere. They may be so absolutely convincing in political and economic matters as to accomplish 'sheer miracles'. This will give them a certain religious affectation so that many people will have no doubt about their exalted mission. Certain well-known phenomena of the present may be seen as precursors of these false prophets. Especially in politics a future development in this direction seems likely to intensify and to be full of surprises. A great difficulty will be that the outstanding abilities of those endowed with supersensory authority cannot be denied; for discernment between Luciferic-Ahrimanic genius and true grace of spirit is not easy.

It is not a question of clumsy manoeuvres of deception, and the Gospel says that even the 'chosen ones' may be deceived by signs and miracles, and for this reason it again and again calls for the utmost care and alertness. The main danger will be in the appearance of personalities presenting themselves as the Christ. Impostors and sick people with religious delusions may of course announce that they are Christ. Such claimants have long existed without causing noticeable danger to Christendom, and they may even in the future find their followers but they need not be taken very seriously as their unimportance is fairly evident. The 'false Christs' of whom the Gospel speaks are of a different calibre. Something special must be involved if they are to cause doubts and temptations for truly serious, convinced and alert Christians. The only thing that could be meant here is that men will come who, through their surpassing spiritual powers, are able to give the impression that something divine is living in them. This possibility does not exist as long as man can draw only on his own human faculties—great as they may be—but it can occur if, as described above, a permeation by Ahrimanic-Luciferic forces is taking place. The false Christs will be people in whom the temporary incarnation of demonic intelligences grows to lasting estrangement, perhaps even for years.

That Christ speaks of many false Christs suggests that their appearance may be interpreted as a prelude to the appearance of the actual Antichrist. The following words from the First Letter of John apply here. 'Children, it is the last hour; and as you have heard that antichrist is coming, so now many antichrists have come; therefore we know that it is the last hour.' (2:18). John distinguishes between a number of antichrists and the Antichrist himself. He will not appear until the many who are active in his spirit have been present to prepare his appearance. In this sense he says, 'This is the spirit of antichrist, of which you have heard that it was coming; and now it is in the world already.' (1 John 4:3).

In the Second Letter of Paul to the Thessalonians we have the most important comment on the Antichrist on which Christendom has always relied. He is described as 'the man of lawlessness ... the son of perdition, who opposes and exalts himself against every so-called god or object of worship, so that he takes his seat in the temple of God, proclaiming himself to be God' (2:3–4). Paul refers to these events as the 'mystery of lawlessness' (2:7) which is already at work but is still restrained; its complete unveiling would come later. He prophesies that Satan-Ahriman will use the power of lies, signs and wonders for the seduction, and that God will send 'strong delusion' to those who have not the love of truth. (2:11).

What, in the end, is the mystery of Antichrist?

The Coming of Antichrist

Ahriman, as a spiritual being of cosmic order, cannot immediately live as man in a physical body on earth. He has at first to become active in the intellectual consciousness of men, then in the permeation of civilization and finally in the temporary incarnation in individuals. Through this progress his aim of an ever-tightening hold over the earth is revealed and this desire points to further physical embodiment. The mystery of evil culminating in the appearance of the Antichrist may be understood as a unique appearance of Ahriman fully incarnate in the physical body of a human being.

If they take it seriously at all, people of our time—which is so naïve in spiritual matters—are inclined to assume that this world-event will show like a sudden magic wonder before the eyes of an astounded mankind. But the cosmic development to which Lucifer and Ahriman are subject, just as much as all other beings, is a tremendous organic process with slowly developing stages. The adversaries cannot interfere at will. They too have to move within the limits set for them by the Godhead. Their realm of influence, although of breathtaking magnitude for us human beings, is not unlimited and they are obliged to forward their work stage by stage. The great crisis that will decide the fate of mankind is being prepared by the demonic powers in their own interest, no less than by the good forces who are serving the divine world and helping humanity. Thus the transient appearances of Ahriman in men must be seen as one of the most important antecedents of the appearance of Antichrist. It cannot be denied, therefore, that declarations of Nero or other historical personalities as Antichrist had a partial basis of truth, for those were predecessors of persons who will become the direct voice of Ahriman. Through them, step by step, he approaches his goal of being able to work in full demonic greatness on earth.

Seers such as John the Divine could foretell these happenings so that humanity would not be totally ignorant and unprepared for the greatest crisis of its spiritual development. Men cannot be spared this crisis, but it is largely given them to fend off the worst of the Antichrist's assault. Nothing would more assist it than human naïvety. Without an understanding of the event of Golgotha and a living connection with the continuing power of the Risen Christ, men would be helpless in face of what is coming.

At that time the divine being of Christ incarnated in the human Jesus of Nazareth. 'And the Word became flesh' (John 1:14). In future this light-filled archetype will be confronted by its dark negative: the incarnation of the demonic in man. Neither event is completely revealed by the visible facts. They are at the same time earthly and supersensory happenings and of an importance reaching far beyond the visible boundaries. Through the Mystery of Golgotha, a divine being entered the earthly world and gave himelf to mankind as a silently active impulse of love, forgoing and sacrificing any display of his own divine power. He does not overwhelm and coerce, but appeals to the free decision of the human will. At the time of the Antichrist's appearance on earth it is certain that the human being will be paralyzed under an Ahrimanic spell: a suggestive display of unheard-of power, a whipping up of all kinds of passions. The two events are characterized by the manner of their appearance. The good does not dominate, it heals. The evil seeks to overpower, and destroys.

In the Gospel, the coming of Antichrist is shown as something that cannot be avoided; it *must* occur, and it overshadows all who live on earth. However it is up to the free choice of each person how he takes this trial and it is very much an open question *who* will overcome it. With sombre words men are reminded to do all in their power to help to wrest a blessing from this irrevocable event: 'Watch and pray . . .' (Matt. 26:41).

Alertness of consciousness and prayerful devotion to the

divine are the two means given to man to turn evil's assault into a victory for the good. In every possible way the dark powers will seek to cloud the faculty of clear thinking and decision. Through the superhuman intelligence at their disposal they will try to keep their own being and aims unrecognized. For one of the strongest weapons of evil is its disguise: it can employ its full power only where it can be hidden. For this reason the adversaries use the most diverse masks and for this reason Ahriman will assume the form of Christ! All Ahriman's previous attempts have had effect because they have not been recognized. Recognition of evil is the beginning of its conquest. Before the image of its own being in the mirror of spiritually healthy thinking, evil must retreat. Watchful insight is one means by which the aims of Ahriman can be defeated. The other is prayer. Not the threadbare praying and pleading which is all that our age, poor in feeling and willing, produces: but the strong prayer rich in faith that welled up within the great men of prayer of the Middle Ages, and must be recovered: the prayer of meditation and devotion, able to implore the grace that gives divine strength, as does the communal prayer at the altar. If the individual learns to understand the depth of the task underlying the simple admonition to watch and pray, he contributes his share in withstanding the Antichrist's assault.

A man could become faint-hearted, and doubtful whether his strength of consciousness and prayer is sufficient, in view of the terror of evil, the gigantic power it commands and the unveiling of the arch-evil that is expected in the Antichrist. If one allowed the thought of evil to dominate, it would indeed be paralysing and take away all hope. True, it would be unrealistic, superficial and dangerous not to want to see the abysses, but it is also true that they are not the only things in this world. The development of evil is always confronted by an increase in the good.

In the same degree as the gates of the underworld are opening, the heavens also open, since in spite of the diversity of its beings, the supersensible world is a unity. The dark powers can rise in strength only because the divine world is near. As the demons were the first to recognize Christ two thousand years ago, and increased their activity in the man possessed (Mark 1:24; 3:11), so each divine revelation is preceded by its shadow: an increase of demonic power. The present unprecedented intensification of evil and the appearance of Antichrist may be evaluated as signs and trials heralding a great revelation of the divine. *The Second Coming of Christ is the event that casts its shadow ahead in the form of Antichrist:* '. . . for that day will not come, unless the rebellion comes first, and the man of lawlessness is revealed, the son of perdition'. (2 Thess. 2:3). All attacks of the demonic are an attempt to cloud this most important spiritual happening. As the evil works 'with all power and with pretended signs and wonders' (2 Thess. 2:9), to rob humanity of its intended blessing, so does the divine world send its helping forces. And as the day of Antichrist is prepared by many influences, assaults and advances, so too the way is prepared for Christ's spiritual return through forerunners, helpers and gifts of the spirit. It may be esteemed one such blessing that, after long darkening of the world by materialism, new paths of spiritual cognition have been prepared in the twentieth century by Rudolf Steiner's Anthroposophy. Through this gift of understanding, the warning call of the Gospel for watchfulness is supported and strengthened in an unforeseen way. A further revelation of the forces preparing for Christ's Second Coming is experienced through the establishment of a new service at the altar. The spiritual gift of the sacraments, which are central to the work of The Christian Community, allows an instreaming of blessing and confirms the words of the Psalm: 'Thou preparest a table before me in the presence

The Coming of Antichrist

of my enemies' (Ps. 23:5). Without invalidating the straightforward, universally human significance of this sentence, it may be understood in the sense that the Godhead erects a 'table of the Lord' in plain view of the adversary. Through the sacrament of communal prayer at the altar, the second demand of the Gospel, 'pray', receives its divine strengthening. Man does not stand alone in the decisive spiritual struggle. The call of the Gospel: 'Watch and pray . . .' is not just a demand that abandons him to his own weakness—at the right hour, help is given for its fulfilment.

The revelation of evil does not have to cause despair. It is confronted by the new revelation of Christ. Man is not going to be spared the struggle for the right decision between Christ and Antichrist in difficult outer and inner battles, but all the spiritual help he may need during this cosmic hour will be given. Freedom of choice imposes responsibilities and trials which have shaken humanity to the core with apocalyptic temptations and cosmic storms. At the same time, this freedom constitutes the nobility and dignity of man. He may feel confirmed therein by God, and trusting in his help can bravely meet the events that are to come.